The Piskey-Purse

' Elves, Urchens, Goblins all, and Little Fairyes.'

'*The ugly little creature sped away, followed by three wee hares.*'

p. 101.

THE PISKEY-PURSE

Legends and Tales of North Cornwall

BY

ENYS TREGARTHEN

Illustrated by
J. LEY PETHYBRIDGE

NEW ORLEANS & NEW YORK

ARABI MANOR

A REBEL SATORI IMPRINT

2024

Published in the United States of America by
Arabi Manor
A Rebel Satori Imprint
www.rebelsatoripress.com

Originally published by Wells Gardner, Darton & Co., Ltd.,
London, 1905.

Foreword copyright 2024 Rebel Satori Press.

Cover photo: Sunset on The Merry Maidens Stone Circle,
Cornwall, United Kingdom by Fahad Almotrif

Paperback ISBN: 978-1-60864-322-6

Arabi Manor Foreword

The Cornish Piskey, or Pixie, holds a special place in the folklore of Cornwall, a county in the southwestern part of England. These mischievous and mysterious creatures have been a part of Cornish legend for centuries, and their presence continues to captivate the imaginations of locals and visitors alike. In this book, Enys Tregarthen explores the legends and folklore of North Cornwall shedding light on the rich tapestry of folklore that has woven them into the cultural fabric of Cornwall.

Originating from the Celtic roots of Cornwall, the Cornish Piskey is believed to be a diminutive, fairy-like entity with a penchant for both playful antics and helpful deeds. While their exact origins remain shrouded in the mists of time, the Piskey's presence is deeply intertwined with the landscape of Cornwall, where they are said to inhabit the rugged moors, ancient woodlands, and secluded valleys. Tales of encounters with these otherworldly beings have been passed down through generations, adding to the enduring allure of the Cornish Piskey.

The characteristics ascribed to the Cornish Piskey vary widely across different accounts and traditions. In some tales, they are described as benevolent guardians of the natural world, delighting in guiding lost travelers to safety and offering assistance to those in need. However, other stories depict them as playful tricksters, capable of leading unwary wanderers astray or causing mild mischief in homes and fields. Despite their mischievous nature, the Piskey is generally viewed with affection and respect, and many Cornish people believe in their existence to this day.

The significance of the Cornish Piskey extends beyond mere folklore, influencing various aspects of Cornish culture, including literature, art, and even tourism. Their enduring presence in local folklore has inspired numerous works of literature and art, making them a beloved symbol of Cornwall's mystical heritage. Additionally, the Piskey has become a popular figure in tourist attractions, with visitors eager to explore the enchanting realms where these mythical beings are said to dwell.

Nellie Sloggett was born in Padstow in 1851 and died in 1923. Writing as Enys Tregarthen and Nellie Cornwall, Sloggett was a popular author and folklorist. She made a significant contribution to preserving and sharing the rich legends and folklore of North Cornwall. Through meticulous research and captivating storytelling, her writings delved into the enigmatic world of the Cornish lore and legend, shedding light on its profound cultural significance and enduring allure. Her work has not only brought these mystical Piskeys to life for readers but has also helped to perpetuate the captivating allure of Cornwall's folklore, ensuring that these cherished stories are passed down to future generations. Sloggett's dedication to preserving and celebrating the folklore of North Cornwall has left an indelible mark on the cultural landscape of the region.

Introduction

THE tales given in this small volume, with one exception, are from North Cornwall, where I have always lived.

The scene of ' The Piskey-Purse ' is from Polzeath Bay (in maps called Hayle Bay, which is *not* its local name), in St. Minver parish. This charming spot was once much frequented by the Piskeys and other fairy folk, and many a quaint story used to be told about them by the old people of that place, which some of us still remember. The spot most favoured by the Piskeys for dancing was Pentire Glaze cliffs, where, alas! half a dozen lodging-houses now stand. But the marks of fairy feet are not, they say, all obliterated, and the rings where Piskeys danced may yet be seen on the great headland of Pentire, and tiny paths called ' Piskey Walks ' are still there on the edge of some of the cliffs.

' The Magic Pail ' is a West Cornwall story, the

scene of which is laid on a moorland between Carn Kenidzhek (the Hooting Carn) and Carn Boswavas, and not a great distance from the once-celebrated Ding Dong tin-mine.

The ancient town of Padstow provides the 'Witch in the Well'; lovely Harlyn Bay, in the parish of St. Merryn, is the scene of 'Borrowed Eyes and Ears'; and the 'Little White Hare' is from the Vale of Lanherne, at St. Mawgan in Pydar.

Readers will gather from these tales that we have several kinds of fairies in Cornwall—the Good Little People, the Merry Little People, and the Bad Little People. To the latter belong the Spriggans, who are spiteful and lovers of money, and who have all the hidden treasures in their keeping. The Merry Little People are the Piskeys and the Nightriders, and are the best known of all the Wee Folk. The Piskeys are always dancing, laughing, and 'carrying on.' Their special delight is in leading the traveller astray, and who is at their mercy till he turns a garment inside out. The Nightriders take horses out of the stable and ride them over the moors and downs when their owners are in bed.

There are many quaint accounts as to the origin of the Cornish fairies. According to one tradition they are the Druids, who, because they opposed Christ-

Introduction

ianity when it was first preached in Cornwall, were made to dwindle in size till they became the Little People they now are. The worst opposers of the Christian Faith dwindled to ants!

Another tradition says that the Wee Folk are the original inhabitants of Cornwall, who lived here long centuries before the Birth Star of the Babe of Bethlehem was seen in the East. In North Cornwall they are still sometimes called the ' little *Ancient* People.'

Whoever the Cornish fairies are, and whatever their origin, they are not without their interest from the folklore point of view, and we hope that these stories about them will be pleasing, not only to Cornish people themselves, but to those who come to visit ' the land outside England.'

I am indebted to my kind publishers for their deep interest in these folklore tales, and to Mr. J. Ley Pethybridge, a Cornishman, for so faithfully depicting many of the scenes referred to.

ENYS TREGARTHEN

Contents

List of Illustrations

List of Illustrations

The Piskey-Purse

Polzeath Bay.

U NDER a hill, and facing Polzeath Bay, a wild, desolate but magnificent porth on the north coast of Cornwall, stood a small stone cottage, thatched with reed, and with tiny casement windows. It was enclosed by a low hedge, also built of stone, which many generations of orange-coloured lichens, pennycakes and moss, had made pleasant to look at and soft to sit on.

I

The Piskey-Purse

The cottage and hedge thus confronting the porth, with its beach of grey-gold sand, commanded the great headland that flanked it on its north side, and leagues and leagues of shining water stretching away to where the sun went down. Three people lived in this cottage—a very old woman called Carnsew, and her two great-grandchildren—Gerna and Gelert.

They were a lonely trio, for they were the only people living at the bay at that time.

The children had nobody but themselves to play with, and nothing much to do all day long save to pick limpets for their Great-Grannie's ducks, and to help her a bit in the houseplace and in the garden, which grew very little except potatoes, cabbages, herbs, and gillyflowers. They never went to school, for there was no school for them to go to, even if their great-grandmother could have afforded to send them, which she could not; but in spite of that, they were not ignorant children, and although they did not know A from B, they knew a great deal about the Small People, or fairies, of which there were many kinds in the Cornish land.

The Great-Grannie having lived ninety odd years in the world, was well up in everything relating to the Small People, or she thought she was, and it was she who told her great-grandchildren about them.

Gerna and Gelert cared most to hear about what they called their own dear Wee Folk—the merry little Piskeys—who, Great-Grannie said, lived in one of the *googs* or caverns down in their bay.

The Piskey-Purse

Piskey Goog, as their particular cavern was called, was half-way down the beach in Great Pentire itself, and just beyond Pentire Glaze Hawn. On the top of the cliff were large Rings, where the merry Little People held their *gammets*, or games, and danced in the moonshine.

The children often sat on the hedge of their cottage to watch the Piskeys dancing, and, as the hedge was in view of Pentire Glaze cliffs, they could hear the Piskeys laughing, which they did so heartily that sometimes Gerna and Gelert could not help laughing too. They could also see their lights— *Piskey-lights* they called them—flashing on the turf until they sometimes wondered if a hundred little dinky*-fires were burning there.

One June evening, when the moon was getting near her full and making everything beautiful, even the dark headland standing grimly out from the soft sky, the Piskeys, as they thought, were again holding their revels on the top of the cliff, and as they danced the Rings seemed one blaze, and their laughter broke more frequently than ever on the quiet of the evening. There was no other sound to be heard save the far-off growl of the sea, for the tide was down.

Gerna and her brother were on the hedge as usual, and as they watched the dark moving figures and the flashing of the little fires they longed that they, too, could join the dancers.

* Tiny.

3   I—2

The Piskey-Purse

When the fun seemed to be at its height, the Piskey-lights went suddenly out, and a weird cry, like the cry of a sea-bird proclaiming a storm, broke on the silence, which so startled the children that they gripped each other's hands in trembling amazement. Then they saw in the moonshine hundreds and hundreds of tiny dark figures, all in a line, on the edge of the cliffs from Pentire Glaze Hawn to the cliff above Piskey Goog, some of whom seemed to be bending over the cavern; and then they disappeared.

The day following, Great-Grannie sent Gelert up to St. Hinver Churchtown, a village three miles from Polzeath, on an errand, and Gerna down to the bay to pick limpets. The little girl had picked half a basketful when she saw a dozen or more Piskey-purses lying by the side of a rock-pool. Leaving her basket near a seaweed-covered rock, she went to get them.

Her Great-Grannie had told her and Gelert that these brown, skin-like things so often found in this bay were used by the Piskeys to keep their gold in, and if they were ever lucky enough to find a Piskey-purse with their coins in it they would be rich as a Spriggan.*

Gerna and her brother never forgot this : not that the dear little maid loved money, or wanted to be rich, for she certainly did not ; but her Great-Grannie did, and so did her brother ; and so, for their sakes, whenever Gerna saw a Piskey-purse she stooped and picked it up to see if it contained any golden pieces.

* Spriggan, a low kind of fairy.

4

The Piskey-Purse

But the only gold she had ever found in them were grains of sand!

When the little girl had picked up all the brown bags she could see, to look into at her leisure, her soft blue eyes were attracted by a light-brown mottled thing half-hidden under a bunch of wet seaweed. Taking it up, she found it was a Piskey-purse, at least *in shape*, but it was of a much lighter colour, and all over it were tiny golden rings, with a halo of silver round each, like rays shooting out from a sun. Its skin was not flat like all the other Piskey-purses she had ever seen. It was quite plump, and rather soft, like a half-ripe gooseberry, and closed at both ends, which was also unusual.

As she was wondering if it were a Piskey-purse, a tiny voice, no bigger than a wren's, only far sweeter, came out of the purse, which so frightened the child that she nearly dropped it.

'Hide me quickly in your pocket,' it said. 'They are coming out on the bar to look for this purse, but please *don't* let them find it.'

Gerna was too terrified to do other than she was asked, and lifting the skirt of her tinker-blue frock, she dropped the mottled purse into the depths of an unbleached pocket tied under her frock.

She had scarcely done so when she saw a tiny kiskey* of a man come out of Piskey Goog, followed by a score of others much like himself.

They all had on three-cornered hats and knee-

* Brown, withered like a twig.

5

The Piskey-Purse

breeches, their tiny sticks of legs were encased in black stockings, and on their feet they wore low-heeled buckled shoes.

Apparently they did not see Gerna, who was standing on the edge of the pool with her pinafore half-full of brown Piskey-purses.

Their little faces, which were not pleasant to look at, for they were brown and withered—much more withered and brown than the Great-Grannie's—were bent on the sand. It was easy to tell, by the way they were turning over every bit of seaweed, that they were searching for something.

As one of the wee Dark Men—it was the first who came out of the goog—turned his face seaward, he caught sight of Gerna standing by the pool.

Instead of his disappearing into the cavern, as Great-Grannie told her the Small People would do when they saw anybody looking at them, he took off his little three-cornered hat and came towards her, and Gerna, poor little maid, was too frightened to run away.

'May I ask what you have got in your pinny' (pinafore), 'which you are holding so tight?' he asked, with what was meant to be a most fascinating smile, but which only terrified her the more.

'Only Piskey-purses, please, little mister,' she gasped, 'which I was a-going to look into when I've got time.'

'What did you hope to find there, eh?'

'Some of the dear little Piskeys' golden money,' answered the child.

6

'*She opened wide her pinafore so that the tiny Brown Man could take them out.*'

The Piskey-Purse

' Did you ?   You are a nice little girl ' (she was a giantess compared with him) ' to want the Small People's gold, and I hope one of the purses has some.   May I look into them for you and see ?'

' Iss, if you like,' cried Gerna ; and, sitting down on the sand, she opened wide her pinafore, so that the tiny Brown Man could take them out, which, however, he did not do.

' The Small People never put anything of value into these common brown things,' he said disdainfully, just glancing at the purses in her lap. ' The bags into which *we* put *our* golden money are much prettier, and are painted all over with golden rings, with dashes of white, like this,' making tiny strokes with his finger on the sand. ' If you ever find such a purse you will indeed be a lucky little maid—that is, if you take it into Piskey Goog and put it on a shelf of rock there, which is what I want you to do.   We value these ring-marked purses more than I can tell you,' he continued, as Gerna did not speak, ' and are greatly troubled when we lose one of them ; we have done so now, and shall never be happy any more until we find it.'

' My dear life !' ejaculated the child.

' In return for your kindness, if you find the bag we have lost and bring it to Piskey Goog, we will give you another something like it, full of gold, and you will be quite rich, and be able to buy anything you want.'

' My dear soul and body !' ejaculated Gerna again.

The Piskey-Purse

'I mean what I say,' continued the man, looking up into the little maid's open face with a glitter in his twinkling black eyes, which were no bigger than a robin's eyes, and not nearly so soft. 'But I warn you that if you *do* find this purse, you must not tell anybody of your great find, but bring it straight to Piskey Goog.'

Whilst he was impressing this upon Gerna, who was getting over her fear of the little Brown Man, she remembered the mottled purse in her pocket, and was on the point of telling him, when a great voice roared out over the bay, and, on looking round, she saw a man called Farmer Vivian coming across the bar.

The great voice, or Farmer Vivian himself, she did not know which, so frightened the Brown Piskey Man that he took to his heels, and in less than a minute he and all the other Little Men had vanished into their cavern.

Gerna was on the point of following him thither, for she was almost certain that the mottled purse she had found was the one they had lost, when a great wave broke over the rock where she was standing, and nearly knocked her down, and she had to run away from the cavern to escape another wave.

As she turned to go back to her limpet-picking, she found the limpet rocks were all covered with the incoming tide; her basket, poised high on a breaker and upside down, was fortunately thrown in on the sands at her feet.

The Piskey-Purse

'Great-Grannie will be terribly put out,' she told herself as she went home, 'and the poor little ducklings will have to go without supper.'

The ancient dame was even more vexed than Gerna thought she would be, and sent her at once to bed, and Gelert had to sit on the hedge alone to watch the Piskeys dancing; but they never appeared on the headland, for all his watching.

As Gerna was undressing, the pocket under her frock began to twitch and shake as if it had St. Vitus's dance. As she hastened to untie it, the little voice she had heard in the mottled purse before the Wee Men came out of the cavern spoke to her again.

'Please take me out of your pocket; I want so much to talk to you.'

The child, though somewhat afraid, did so, and held the bag carefully in her hand.

'I cannot tell you how thankful I feel that you did not take me to Piskey Goog, as that little Brown Man asked you to do.'

'Did you hear what he said?' asked Gerna, greatly surprised.

'Every word; and I was so afraid you would tell him you had found me. It would have been too dreadful if you had, especially after they dropped me by accident over the cliff, as they did, and haven't been able to find me since.'

'However did you get into this purse?' asked the child.

'Hager, the King of the Spriggans, put me in here

and sealed me up, so that I should not get out,' said the little voice.

' Whatever for ?'

' Because I wouldn't marry him, and because he was afraid somebody else I loved was going to marry me.'

' He can't be a very nice king,' said Gerna. ' I am glad I didn't take the purse to the cavern, as you are inside. You know, don't you, that the little brown kiskey of a man promised they would give me a bag full of gold if I took this purse to their place. Will they ?'

' It all depends,' answered the little voice. ' The Spriggans—all those little Dark Men you saw on the sands were Spriggans—are dreadful storytellers, and they never keep their word unless they are obliged to. If they cannot get this purse without having to pay heavily for it, they will give you what they offered. Do you want to be rich, dear little maid ?' it asked anxiously.

' *I* don't one bit,' returned the child truthfully ; ' but my Great-Grannie and my brother Gelert do. If they were to know that the little Brown Man had promised to give me a bag of gold if I take this one to Piskey Goog, Great-Grannie would *make* me take it. We are very poor—poor as a coot, she says.' As the small voice in the purse was silent : ' If I don't take you to the goog, will *you* give me some of the dear Little People's golden money ?'

' I have no gold to give,' said the voice very sadly. ' And if I had, I would not like to give it you, for it would not bring you real happiness. But if you take me down to the cavern, as the Spriggan suggested, you will break my heart. Hager,* who is even crueller than his name, will never let me escape from him any more.'

'But I wasn't going to take *you* to the goog,' said Gerna. 'I should let you out first, of course.'

'It is very kind of you to say so,' said the little voice, with a tremble in it. 'But you would not be able to open this purse, which, by the way, is not a purse at all, but a prison.'

'I guess I could,' cried the child. 'My hands are ever so strong, and if they can get limpets off the rocks, they can open this tiny little thing, I'm sure. I'll open it now, this very minute.'

Her strong young fingers began tugging at the end of the bag, but to her surprise she could not open it.

After working for ten minutes or more, she gave up in despair.

'I told you so,' said the tiny voice sadly. 'Much stronger fingers than yours could not open this prison-bag, and no knife, however sharp, could cut its skin.'

'Why could it not?' asked the little maid.

'Because a spell has been worked upon it,' the wee voice answered.

'I don't know what you mean,' said Gerna.

'When Hager put me here,' explained the voice,

* Hager is Celtic-Cornish for cruel, foul, ugly, etc.

The Piskey-Purse

'he was so afraid the dear Little People, and those who loved me, would discover where he had put me, and find out a way to release me, that he made it impossible by an evil spell that anybody—even himself—should be able to set me free for ninety-nine years three hundred and sixty-five days, unless a very poor little girl could be found who had no love of gold in her soul, nor any greed for riches, and who, out of the deep pity of a kind little heart, would be willing to carry me for love's sake, in the dead of night, through a great bog haunted by hobgoblins, over a lonely moor to where a Tolmên* stands, and pass me three times through the Tolmên's hole before the sun rises, and then lay me on its top, so that the first ray of the rising sun might smite upon the bag. This will break the spell and set me free.'

'What a terrible lot for a little maid to do!' cried Gerna. 'I don't believe one will ever be found to do all that, however kind she is.'

'That is just what Hager believed,' said the voice sadly. 'And yet I was once hopeful that such a dear little child would be found, or rather would find this purse with its helpless prisoner inside, and take compassion on me. But as the long years dragged on, and no such little maiden came to my help, hope died within me, and I was in utter

* A Tolmên, or Holed Stone, is one of the antiquities of Cornwall, and many superstitions have been connected with it, such as passing weakly children through its hole, in the belief they will get stronger.

despair, until *you* discovered me half hidden under some seaweed, picked me up, and brought me hither. And now hope has begun to revive in my heart again.'

' Have you been in this prison-purse a long time ?' asked Gerna, who dimly felt that the poor little prisoner was appealing to her pity.

' A very long time,' sighed the little voice—' *one hundred years all but a few days.*'

' My goodness gracious !' exclaimed the little Cornish maid in great amazement. ' How terrible old you must be—older even than my Great-Grannie, who is ever so much past ninety.'

' I suppose I am old, as you count age,' said the little voice, in which Gerna detected a laugh.

' Have you really been in this bag ninety-nine years ?' she asked, not being able to get over her surprise.

' Yes ; and I am grieved to say the hour for my release has almost come. Before the birth of the new moon, which is on Friday next, Hager will take me out, if no child before that time carries me over the bog and moor, and passes me through the Tolmên.'

' Was it only 'cause you wouldn't marry that old Spriggan king you got put into this prison ?' asked Gerna.

' Yes, that was the only reason,' answered the little voice. ' I happened to be beautiful, you see, and because of my beauty he stole me away from my own dear little True Love, who was just going to marry me. If it ends, as I fear it will, in his getting me into his power again, I and my True Love will break our hearts.'

'But I shouldn't think anybody would want to marry you now, if you are so old as you say you are,' cried Gerna, with all a child's candour, thinking of her shrivelled, toothless old great-grandmother.

'And yet Hager, in spite of my age, is waiting impatiently for the waning of the moon to marry me,' said the little voice, with another sigh. 'I overheard him talking about it to some of his people, and what grand doings they would have then, and how they would send an invitation to all the dear Little People—my own True Love included—to come to the wedding.'

'What a horrid person he must be !' cried Gerna indignantly. 'Why ever didn't your little True Love come and take you away ?'

'He can't, because of the spells Hager worked upon this bag.'

'Haven't you seen your little True Love all those long years ?' asked the child.

'Not once. But I thought I heard his voice when the little Brown Man was telling you to bring the ring-marked purse to Piskey Goog.'

'There was nobody on the beach except those little Dark Men searching for this purse and Farmer Vivian,' said Gerna. 'Farmer Vivian is a great big

man, and lives up at Pentire Glaze Farm. He is
very kind, and he do love all the Little People
dearly.'

'How do you know he does?' asked the little voice
eagerly.

'My Great-Grannie told me he did, and *she* do know.
This little cottage of ours belongs to him, and he
al'ays talks to her about the Wee Folk when she
goes up to his house to pay the rent. There!
Great-Gran is calling up the stairs to ask if I'm in
bed. I shall have to put 'ee back into my big
pocket now. I hope you won't mind.'

'Not one bit. The only thing I do mind is being
given into Hager's power. You won't take me to
Piskey Goog, whatever the little Brown Man offers
you, will you, dear?'

'Not unless Great-Grannie finds out I've got you
an' makes me,' said the child, putting the purse very
carefully into the unbleached pocket. 'I hope she
won't go looking into it when she comes up to
bed.'

'Can't you hide the pocket somewhere?' asked
the little voice anxiously.

'I can put it into the big chest here by the
window,' said Gerna, looking around the mean little
chamber, which was very bare. 'A storm washed it
in on the bar last winter, and Great-Gran don't keep
nothing in it but her best clothes.'

'Then put me into the chest,' piped the little
voice. 'And please come and take me out to-morrow

as soon as you can. It cheers me to hear the voice of a friend, and I believe you are a true friend, you dear little maid!'

The child dropped the pocket into the great sea-chest very quickly, for the ancient dame again called up the stairs to ask if she were in bed, and then came up to see if she were.

Great-Grannie did not get up until quite late the next day, and when she did she sent Gerna to the beach to pick limpets for the ducks, and Gelert to weed the small potato plot at the back of the cottage, a work he hated doing.

When the little girl got to the bay the tide was only half-way down, and it was ever so long before she could get near the limpet rocks. But as soon as the tide let her she began her limpet-picking, and never looked round once.

Her basket was half full when she heard a sharp little voice behind her.

' Have you found the purse I told you of?'

' I haven't looked yet to-day,' said the child, without glancing round. ' I lost all my limpets yesterday through picking up Piskey-purses, an' my Great-Grannie was ever so cross. She sent me to bed without any supper; an' the poor little ducks had to go without their supper too.'

' I *am* so sorry,' said the little Brown Man, climbing the rock to be on a level with her face; ' but I would not let such a small matter as that prevent *me* from looking for that purse with its gold ring markings. Your Great-Grannie will never be vexed with you any more when you have found it, and receive another one full of the Small People's gold in exchange.'

'How did you come to lose your purse?' asked the child, anxious to hear what he would say.

'Unfortunately, I took it with me a night or two ago to the cliff above our dwelling-place, where we have our games, and by a terrible misfortune I dropped it over the cliff. I and my relations have been looking for it ever since. I have come here to-day to renew the offer I made yesterday. You would like to be rich, wouldn't you?'

'We are terrible poor!' said the child evasively —'the poorest people in St. Minver parish, Great-Grannie said.'

'Are you really, you poor things?' said the little Brown Man kindly. '. Then, in that case I will double my reward if you find the purse. I will give you two purses full of the Small People's golden money instead of only one. It must, however, be brought to Piskey Goog before the next new moon, and as the present one is in her last quarter, there is not much time to lose, is there?'

'No,' said the child, still going on with her limpet-picking.

'Won't you go and look for it now?' asked the little Brown Man, with a hint of impatience in his voice. 'The tide will be on the flow again soon, and your chance for to-day will be gone.'

The Piskey-Purse

'I must fill my basket with limpets first,' said
Gerna; 'Grannie raises ducks to sell to the gentry,
and we can't afford for them to lose a meal, she
says.'

'You are like a limpet yourself; there is no moving
you against your will,' cried the little man, scowling,
'and——'

What else he would have said there was no knowing, for Farmer Vivian appeared on the sands at
that moment, and shouted across the gray-gold bar,
and this caused the little Piskey Man to take to his
heels and run into his cavern.

Gerna did not stay on the beach after the wee
Brown Man had disappeared—she felt afraid somehow—and she went home with only half a basketful
of limpets. This so put out Great-Grannie that she
vowed she would send her down to the porth again
to find more, if one of her precious ducklings hadn't
taken it into its head to have a fit, which so bewildered her that she sent Gelert instead !

What with the sick duckling to attend to, and
other little chores the child had to do for the ancient
dame, she had not a minute to steal up to the little
chamber.

When at last she thought she was free, Gelert
rushed into the cottage all excitement.

'What *do* you think?' he cried, 'the dear little
Piskey Men are out on the sands looking for a
Piskey-purse. They have lost one, they told me,
and whoever finds it and takes it into Piskey Goog

shall have a purse full of the Small People's golden money.'

'You don't mean for to say so?' exclaimed the old woman. 'To think of it now! Go along, both of 'ee,' glancing at Gerna, 'an' search for that purse until you do find it.'

'I've searched and searched till I'm tired,' said the boy, 'an' I would have gone on searching if the old sea wasn't tearing in like mad.'

'Oh dear, what a pity!' cried the Great-Grannie. 'We must *all* go an' look for that purse to-morrow. I wouldn't have us lose our chance of being rich for anything. Now,' turning to Gerna, 'make haste an' get our suppers, for the boy must be as hungry as a hedger after such work.'

When the supper was ready, and as they were eating, Gelert remarked:

'I forgot to tell you, Great-Grannie, that the little Brown Men told me it was noised about that Farmer Vivian is going to sell all his land—this little cottage too—and that we are to be turned out.'

'That is the wishtest * news I've heard this longful time,' wailed the old woman. 'There isn't another cottage down here, and all the little houses up to Trebetherick an' Churchtown is more rent than I could ever pay.'

'We shall be able to live in a great big house—the biggest house in the parish—when we've found that

* Saddest.

The Piskey-Purse

purse and got the other with the golden pennies, the little Piskey Man told me,' said the boy. 'The money will come just when we most want it—won't it, Great-Gran dear ?'

'It will,' chuckled

' " That is the wishtest news I've heard." '

the ancient dame ; 'an' we must give ourselves no rest till we find that purse.'

* * * * *.

'I feared you had forgotten me,' said the sweet wee voice in the Piskey-bag an hour later, when Gerna had taken it out of the chest.

'I hadn't forgotten you,' said the child a little sadly ; 'but I couldn't come before, 'cause——'

The Piskey-Purse

'Because what?' asked the little voice anxiously.
'You have not come to give me into the power of
the Spriggans, have you?'

'Not now, but I am afraid I shall have to,' said
Gerna.

And she then told her how the little Brown Man
had come to her again, and how he had doubled his
offer if she brought the lost purse to the goog. She
also told her all the news Gelert had brought up
from the beach, and of Farmer Vivian selling his
cottage.

'There isn't a word of truth about his selling your
cottage,' said the little voice indignantly. 'He is
far too kind to turn an old woman and two little
children like you out of your home. It is because
he is good that the Spriggans are afraid of him and
speak of him so unkindly.'

'But if it should be true,' persisted Gerna, 'will
you give me a purseful of golden money if I don't
take you to the goog?'

'How quickly you forget, child! I told you but
yesterday that I had no gold to give you,' said the
little voice. 'Surely *you* do not love money more
than you do kindness and pity? And you are going
to commit an unkind deed—for it will be an unkind
deed if you sell me for gold. Woe is me!'

'But the purse belongs to the Spriggan King,' said
Gerna, as if to excuse herself. 'I shall be only
giving him what belongs to him.'

'That is quite true. But *I* do not belong to him;

The Piskey-Purse

I belong to my Mammie and Daddy and my own
little True Love, whom I shall never, never see
again if you take me to Piskey Goog. And I shall
be dead to them for ever and ever and ever !'

'Then I won't let those nasty little Dark People
have 'ee, whatever they do offer,' cried the child. 'I
only wish I could take 'ee over that bog an' moor
you told me of to the Tolmên.'

'A wish is father to the deed,' said the little voice
somewhat more cheerfully. 'If you really desire to
do that act of pity,' it added, after a pause, 'you
have not much time to lose, for the moon is on the
wane, and there are only three clear days to the birth
of the new moon.'

'I wish I wasn't afraid of being out alone in the
dark,' said the child, shuddering. 'I am a wisht
coward when it is dark. So I'm afraid I shall never
be brave enough to take 'ee to the Tolmên, though
I want to, dreadful. But I'll never let the Spriggans
have 'ee, dear,' she added, greatly distressed, as a
groan terrible in its despair came out of the bag.
'Don't 'ee make so wisht a sound. It do make me
sad to hear 'ee.'

'I can't help it,' said the wee voice, which was as
full of tears as ever a voice could be. 'Not even
love can keep me from the Spriggans after the moon
is born. All power to resist them will be gone, and
they can come into this cottage unseen by human
eyes and take me away. They suspect where I am
now, and are only afraid I have discovered a child

who is not only no lover of money, but who is kind enough to take me to the Tolmên.'

'Whatever will 'ee do !' cried Gerna, tears welling to her eyes. 'I don't believe I shall be happy any more if I know those ghastly little Spriggans have 'ee.'

'I don't believe you would, you dear little maid.'

'I tell 'ee what,' cried the child, making a big resolve: 'I *will* take—— There! Great-Grannie is coming up the stairs. Good-night till to-morrow.'

The ancient dame was up with the sun the next day, and made Gerna and Gelert get up too, that no time might be lost in looking for the Piskey-purse. She would hardly give them time to eat their breakfast, so greedy was she to have the Small People's golden money.

As she was taking down her sunbonnet, she knocked over a heavy piece of wood, which fell on her big toe, and it hurt her so badly that, much to her vexation, she had to let the children go without her.

The tide was in when they got down to the bay, and so smooth and still was it that 'it couldn't wash up anything, even if it wanted to,' said Gelert crossly.

He turned over all the seaweed at high-water mark, but saw nothing except sea-fleas.

When the tide was far enough down, Gerna went all over the beach with her brother; but as she had already found the lost purse, she picked up shells instead.

'I don't b'lieve you want to find the Piskey-purse,

The Piskey-Purse

Gerna Carnsew,' growled Gelert, when he saw what she was doing. ' I don't b'lieve you want to have the Small People's golden pieces one little bit.'

' I didn't say I did,' cried Gerna, which made the boy so angry that he went off to the other side of the bar to look for the purse alone.

Gerna was stooping to pick up a shell, of which there were many on the sands to-day, when the little Brown Man came up to her, doffed his three-cornered hat, and grinned into her face.

' Have you found our lost purse yet ?' he asked. ' The time for finding it is up the day after to-morrow.'

' Whatever do you mean, little mister ?'

' What I say, and that your chance of being wealthy will be gone. Are you looking for the precious bag now ?'

' My Great-Grannie sent me and Gelert down here to look for it,' said the child evasively. ' Gelert is over there looking,' again sending her glance across the bar, which was particularly beautiful to-day with reflected clouds.

' I know he is, and he seems much more anxious to find the purse than you are. Perhaps our offer, great as it was, is not sufficiently tempting. If it isn't '—looking keenly into the child's sweet face— ' we will treble our reward. Three purses full of the Wee Folks' golden money will we give you if you bring us the bag. It will be more than enough to buy all the land in your parish, including your own dear little cottage, should it ever be sold.'

The Piskey-Purse

' Will it really ?' cried Gerna, deeply impressed, and for the first time in her innocent young life the desire to be rich came into her unselfish little soul.

' Yes ; and you will be a very great lady indeed,' said the small Dark Man, with an evil laugh, seeing he had gained a point—'greater even than Lady Sandys, who lives up at St. Minver Churchtown.'

He might have said many more things to entice the poor little maid's envy ; but just then a great voice above their heads startled them, and, looking up, Gerna saw Farmer Vivian on the top of Tristram, a hill facing Pentire Glaze.

The Spriggan took to his heels at once, and there was a helter-skelter amongst all the Little Men, whom she had not seen on the sands until then, and one and all rushed into Piskey Goog, as if a regiment of soldiers were after them.

Gelert continued his search for the purse until the sea flowed in again, and Gerna sat on a rock picturing to herself what the Churchtown folk would say to her when she bought all the land in the parish, and became a person of even greater importance than Lady Sandys. As she was enjoying all this wealth in anticipation, it suddenly rushed upon her at what price she would buy her riches—the happiness of a poor little helpless thing in a Spriggan's prison—and she felt so ashamed of herself that the desire for gold died within her, and such pity for her little friend came in its place that she was now quite determined

The Piskey-Purse

to take the bag over the bog country to the moor where the Tolmên was, cost her what it might.

When the children came home, Great-Grannie was all eagerness to know if the purse were found, and when Gelert told her it was not, and that Gerna had been looking for shells instead of the lost Piskey-purse, her anger knew no bounds, and she smacked the poor little maid, and once more sent her supperless to bed.

' I wish all the Spriggans' gold would be swallowed up in the sea,' said poor Gerna, as she went up to the little bed-chamber. ' Great-Grannie was never vexed with me before that Dinky Man wanted to make me rich with his golden pieces. 'Tis better to be poor an' contented, I reckon, than to be rich and be miserable.'

The ancient dame, finding her toe getting worse, followed her small great-granddaughter upstairs, and as she did not go down again that night, Gerna had no chance of speaking to the little prisoner. Nor had she the next morning, for she was kept so busy, what with bathing Great-Grannie's injured toe, and all the other odds and ends of things she had to do before going down to the bay, that she had not a minute to herself until bedtime.

The old woman, in her desire for gold, no longer considered the voracious appetites of her numerous ducks, and told the children that, as the finding of that lost purse was of such great importance, the limpet-picking must stand over until the purse was found.

The Piskey-Purse

Gelert was delighted to be relieved of an uncongenial task, and went off to search for the purse with a light heart; but Gerna, not wanting to go to the beach at all, begged to stay at home, which made Great-Grannie so cross that she said she was not to come back until she had found it.

Either the clock had gone wrong or the old woman's brain, for it was much later than she thought, and when the children got down to the bay the sea was rushing up the sands at such a terrible speed that the time for searching was very short. It had surrounded the rocks where the limpets clung when they got there, and was almost up to Piskey Goog.

Gelert went to the other side of the bay at once, leaving Pentire side to Gerna. But as the little maid knew there was no other purse to find than the one she had found, she began again to pick up shells. There were very lovely shells on the sands to-day, all the colours of the rainbow—in fact, they looked as they lay in the eye of the sun as if they had fallen from the sky. As the child was stooping to pick them up, out of the cavern came a troop of little Brown Men, with the Wee Man who had always spoken to her at the head.

He made at once for the child.

' Picking up shells again!' he cried, ' and all those purses of gold awaiting you there in the goog! Why, I am beginning to think you do not want to be rich. Do you?'

The Piskey-Purse

' I did issterday,* but I don't one little bit *now*,' said the child, turning her frank gaze full upon the little Dark Man's upturned face.

' What !' he cried, looking as black as a thunder-cloud, ' you don't mean to tell me that you are going to miss the great chance of having three purses full of the Wee Folks' golden money ?'

' Iss, I do,' said the little maid. ' I don't want even *one* piece of your old golden money, *little Mister Spriggan !*'

If the cliff towering above them had tumbled down upon him the little Dark Man could not have looked more crushed. Then he scowled all over his face, shook his scrap of a fist at her, and yelled :

' I know *now* that you found the purse we lost, and that the little voice within it—*it is nothing more than a voice, remember*—has bewitched you as it has others, and that it does not want you to be rich, happy, and great as we do. You will be sorry all your days you have lost your opportunity to be rich, and you will find you cannot even keep the thing which you have found.'

There was a heavy ground sea that day, and the waves were so huge that Gerna had to go farther up the beach out of their reach, and when she turned to see what the Dinky Men were doing, she saw them all slinking into Piskey Goog like whipped dogs.

Great-Grannie was in no better temper than she had been the previous day at her great-grand-

* Yesterday.

children's failure ; and when she asked if Gerna had been looking for the purse, and Gelert said ' No,' she was so vexed and cross, she not only thumped the child, but sent her upstairs to stay the rest of the day.

The poor little maid felt so miserable that she did not take out the purse and talk to the prisoner for ever so long ; but when she did she told her all she had said to the wee Dark Man.

' Did you really say all that to his face—refuse his gold and call him a Spriggan ?' cried the little voice in amazement.

' I did,' said Gerna ; ' an' he did look terrible, sure 'nough.'

' I don't wonder ! I am sure now you are brave enough to take me through the bog and over the moor to the Tolmên. Will you, dear little maid ?'

' I want to, if I can,' said the child. ' But I don't know the way to the Tolmên. There is no Tolmên anywhere near here that I know of.'

' There is one, though nobody seems to know of it, away towards the sunrising, near where a great Tor rises up against the sky,' said the little voice quite cheerfully. ' I do not know the way to it myself, but there is a *pair of Shoes* which do, and they can take any person on whose feet they are over the worst bog that ever was.'

' What wonderful shoes !' cried Gerna. ' Where are they ?'

' Farmer Vivian has them,' said the little prisoner,

with something in her voice Gerna did not understand.
'They were given him by one of the Small People.
The next time you go down to the beach and see
him there, ask him for these shoes, and *if* they fit
you I shall know for certain that *you* are the little
maid who can save me.'

'Hush!' whispered Gerna. 'Great-Gran is clop-
ping up the stairs, an' I must pop into bed afore she
comes.'

'Take me into bed with you,' whispered back the
little voice, 'and hide me in the folds of your bed-
gown.'

When Gerna was sound asleep, the ancient dame
began to look into every corner of the little chamber,
as if she, too, were searching for something. She
turned out all the things, even the child's pockets,
took everything out of the great sea-chest, muttering
to herself as she did so; and then she went to the
bed where Gerna slept, and turned her over on her
side, and felt under the clothes and the pillow.

'I was wrong; she ent a-got the purse,' she said
aloud to herself, 'an' I thought she had. Aw, dear!
I'm afraid we shall never have that bag an' the
Small People's money.'

And then she undressed and got into bed.

But the old woman could not sleep a wink that
night, and only dozed off when Gerna awoke.

The child had only time to drop her little friend
into the chest before Great-Grannie was wide awake
again and getting up to dress.

The Piskey-Purse

At the flow of the tide the children were again hurried off to the beach to search for the lost Piskey-purse, the old dame loudly lamenting that she was not able to go with them, owing to the hurt to her toe.

The tide was in, and whilst they waited for it to go down, Farmer Vivian came across the bar, and Gelert, seeing him coming towards them, made off.

'How is it you haven't been picking limpets lately?' asked the farmer, with a kindly smile, looking down at Gerna.

'Great-Grannie ordered us to look for a Piskey-purse instead,' said the little maid dolefully.

Then she remembered what the little voice had asked her to do if she saw Farmer Vivian.

'Yes,' he said, in answer to her question, 'I have such a pair of Shoes, and, odd to say, I have them in my pocket. What do you want them for?'

'To see if they will fit me, please, sir. May I have them now and try them on?'

'You may, certainly; but I am afraid they are far too small even for your little feet.'

He dipped his hand into his coat-pocket, and, taking out a tiny pair of moss-coloured Shoes, he gave them to the child.

'Why, they are dolly's shoes!' she cried; 'only big enough for the Small People's feet. I am terribly disappointed.'

'Are you? Well, never mind; just see if they will fit you.'

The Piskey-Purse

'I will, just for fun,' laughed Gerna; and, putting one of them to her bare foot, to her unspeakable amazement it began to stretch, and in a minute it was on!

'Well, I never!' cried Farmer Vivian, and his great voice was so full of delight that it roared out all over the bar, even louder than Giant Tregeagle, whose roar of rage is still sometimes heard on St. Minver sandhills. 'The Shoe has stretching powers, it seems. Try to get on its fellow.'

Gerna quickly did so, and was as proud as a hen with a brood of chicks as she stared at her feet.

'You will have to keep them now,' said the farmer, lowering his big voice to such gentleness and sweetness that she would have thought it was her own little friend at home in the sea-chest if she had not known it wasn't. 'A dear little lady gave them to me to keep until I should find *somebody* they would fit, and I have waited a very long time for that somebody. With the Shoes she gave me a Lantern, which she said must be given with the Shoes;' and once more diving into his pocket, he fished out the tiniest lantern Gerna had ever seen. 'Just big enough,' he said, 'to light home a benighted dumbledory' (bumblebee); and he went away laughing towards the cliffs.

Gerna kept on the Shoes till the tide was down to Piskey Goog, when she took them off and put them into her underskirt pocket with the dinky Lantern.

The sands were strewn with Piskey-purses to-day

34

The Piskey-Purse

nstead of shells, and as it gave her something to do, she picked up as many as she could see ; and when the tide had gone down to Pentire Hawn, she went near there and sat on a rock.

' " *See if they will fit you.*" '

So occupied was she with looking into the purses, and asking herself whether she ever could take the poor little imprisoned fairy across the bog country that night—for she knew it would have to be to-night if she took her at all—that she forgot all about the tide, which by this time had reached its lowest ebb, and was flowing in again.

The sea grew rough as it turned, and began to rush up the great beach and beat on the outer rocks with a terrible roar.

When Gerna had glanced into the last of her purses she looked about her, and found to her consternation that the sea was a long way up the bar, and the rock on which she sat was almost surrounded by angry water.

It was now quite impossible for her to get to the sands, and the only place not cut off by the sea was a tiny cove—a mere gash in the cliff midway between the two hawns, Pentire and Pentire Glaze. As it was, it was her only place of safety—at least, for a time—and she went to it at once, and sat down, white and frightened, under the cliff that towered darkly above her.

After a few minutes she stood up and shouted with all her might for someone to come to her help, but her shouts were drowned in the loud thunder of the breakers. She shouted until she was hoarse— for she did not want to be drowned, poor child, and she knew there was no way out of the cove except by the cliff, which it was quite impossible for her to climb—and then she again sat down and wept bitterly.

As she was crying and sobbing, a strange noise above her made her look up, and there in a tiny hole in the face of the cliff a few feet above her head she saw the grinning face of a little Dark Man!

'You are caught in a trap,' he said, with a cough, 'and you will surely be drowned if *we* do not come to your help.'

'Will you help me, dear little Mister Spriggan?' cried Gerna, hope dawning in her eyes.

'Yes, if you will bring back to our goog, when the sea goes out, that precious purse which we know you have found.'

'I cannot do that, 'cause I promised I wouldn't, whatever happened,' said the child, greatly distressed.

'" Will you help me, dear little Mister Spriggan ?"'

'Oh, then in that case we will leave you to the mercy of the sea ! Of course, it will drown you, and a good thing too, for it will prevent your doing what

The Piskey-Purse

the voice asked you to do. We shall have the bag and *it* in our hands again to-morrow, whilst you will make a dainty dish for the fishes' supper!' and the stone clicked and the ugly little face disappeared.

'Hello! What are you doing down there, and the waves breaking all around you?' cried a voice far up the cliff, and, turning her tearful gaze upwards, Gerna saw kind Farmer Vivian—who looked almost as small as one of the Wee Folk from that great height—looking down upon her. 'A very good thing I gave you those dinky Shoes this morning. Put them on quickly. There is not a moment to lose. In the cliff to your right you will find some steps cut out of the rock. They are very small indeed, but quite large enough for those little green Shoes to climb up on.'

Gerna hastened to obey, and she saw on the face of the cliff a tiny winding stairway. She put her feet on the first stair, and found herself going up and up without fear, and she was soon at the top of the cliff, standing by Farmer Vivian's side.

'There you are, as right as the Small People's change!' said he, with a smile in his eyes, which were as blue as the sea itself, and oh! so gentle and kind. 'Don't take off your Shoes until you have passed all the Piskey Rings, or Spriggan Traps, or whatever they are,' he said, as Gerna turned her face towards her cottage. 'Pentire is full of them to-day—all made since last night, and all the colour of your dear little Shoes.'

The Piskey-Purse

'You can't step anywhere without putting your feet on a Ring,' Gerna said to herself, as she hurried home over the great headland. On every Ring she stepped she felt she must stop to dance like a Piskey. And she was not sure, but she thought she saw little dark faces grinning horribly at her from every Ring she passed over.

Great-Grannie was much upset when she heard what dangers her little great-granddaughter had been exposed to, for Gelert had come home with the news a few minutes before that she was drowned, as he could not see her anywhere!

The fright the old woman received showed her how wrong it was to covet the Small People's money, and she gave Gerna a basinful of hot bread-and-milk, and told her she could go to bed if she liked.

The child was worn out with all she had gone through, and went upstairs quite early, as she wanted to rest before taking the little prisoner to the Tolmên that night.

She did not undress before she had taken the ring-marked purse out of the chest once more, and told her wee friend of all that had happened and what she had gone through.

'I don't believe I should ever have got up that great cliff but for those dinky Shoes,' she added when she had told all; 'nor over Pentire Glaze.'

'I am certain you wouldn't,' said the wee voice. 'The Spriggans were all about the cliffs and head-land, but they were powerless to hinder your going

39

with those Shoes on your feet. You won't be afraid to take me over the bog now, will you, dear little maid?'

'No, that I shan't,' said Gerna; 'an' I'm a-going to do it to-night. But I must have a bit of sleep first. I hope I shall wake in time, an' that Great-Grannie won't miss me till I get back.'

'She won't miss you,' assured the little voice. 'The excitement she has suffered lately has exhausted her, and she will sleep until you are back in your own little bed again. Take me into bed with you, and put me close under your chin, and when the time is up for us to start I will tickle until I wake you.'

The child was soon in a deep slumber, and it seemed to her she had only just fallen asleep when she felt something tickling her neck.

'Dress quickly!' cried the little voice close to her ear. 'But before you do, let me *impress* on you once more that I can never repay you for your kindness, and that all you do for me you must do out of the purest pity and love, and for nothing else. So if you have any hankering after the Little People's gold, your journey is sure to end in failure. For the Spriggans, in spite of the Shoes and the Lantern Farmer Vivian gave you, will prevent your reaching the Tolmên, and will make you give me back into their hands, and thrust upon you the golden pieces they have so often offered you, but which will only bring you trouble.'

The Piskey-Purse

' I don't want anything for taking you to the place where you are to be set free,' said Gerna simply. ' I am doing it 'cause I love you, an' 'cause I am terribly sorry for you and your little True Love, an' I don't want that wicked Hager to make you marry him.'

' Then let us make haste and go,' said the little voice, trembling with gladness. ' Put the Shoes on your feet before you leave the chamber, and the Lantern and me into the bosom of your frock.'

There was no moon, and Gerna had to dress in the dark. It was soon done, and, with the moss-green Shoes on her feet, the ring-printed bag and the wee Lantern close to her heart, she went down the stairs and out into the night.

There was not a sound to be heard save a weird cry somewhere away on Pentire, which the little voice coming up from the bosom of her frock said was Hager howling because his subjects were telling him that he must now give up all hope of ever taking to wife his poor little prisoner. ' You must not be afraid of whatever sounds you hear,' continued the little voice.

' Are we going the right way ?' asked Gerna. For the Shoes were taking them up a rough, steep road behind their cottage.

' Yes, quite right ; the Shoes know the way—trust them for that ! Don't worry about anything ; only hold me as close as you can to your warm little heart. We shall have to warm each other when we come to the bog country. It is bitterly cold there.'

The Piskey-Purse

On and on Gerna went with her precious burden, through long lanes, up and down steep hills, over sandy commons and furze-brakes, and so fast that she could not have spoken even if she wanted to!

At last she drew near the bog lands, lying flat between two high Tors.

'It's terribly cold here,' she said, when the Shoes stuck in the ground for a minute, 'and ever so dark, except where there are little lights shining out of the dark like cats' eyes!' and she began to shiver with cold and fear.

'Don't be afraid, dear child,' said the sweet little voice, in which there was no sadness now. 'The hobgoblins are out in the bog, and as they are near relations of the Spriggans, they are hand in glove with them. The Spriggans feared you would pass over this bog to-night, and have set their relations to watch. But they are not so clever as they thought themselves. They know you have the Shoes, but they don't dream you possess that wee Lantern too.'

'Is the Lantern any good?' asked Gerna in surprise. 'Farmer Vivian said it was only big enough to light home a benighted dumbledory.'

'It was a joke about the dumbledory,' laughed the little voice. 'It can do much more than that. It has the power of making you invisible, and its light will, if you hold it on the little finger, shine in on your heart and keep it warm.'

'What wonderful things there are nowadays!' exclaimed the child.

'*The Shoes began to take her over that dreadful bog.*'

The Piskey-Purse

' Aren't there ?' cried the little voice, with another happy laugh. 'The Lantern will not only give warmth if so held, and cloak you from the hobgoblins and wicked Spriggans, but will also give you courage, which you will need crossing this bog country.'

It was well Gerna was told all this before the Shoes began to take her over that dreadful bog. The mists rose thick and cold as she advanced, and crept over her with such chilling power that she felt as cold as a conkerbell,* she told herself. And the countless little lights, or eyes, or whatever they were, were horrid, and seemed to glaze † at her whichever way she looked. There were groans and sighs, too, which filled her with a nameless terror, and but for the cheerful little voice, which every now and again told her not to be afraid, and the white, clear shining of the tiny Lantern, she would have turned back.

By the time the bog was crossed, which she afterwards learned was by a narrow causeway, just wide enough for two small feet to walk on, she was chill to the very bone and terribly tired.

It was well on towards the sunrising by this time, and there was yet that wild moor to cross before she reached the Tolmên, and she was afraid she would never be able to reach it in time.

She was growing more and more weary every minute, and the Shoes, although they could guide and take her over the most difficult places, did not seem to be able to give her strength.

* Icicle.   † To stare hard.

The Piskey-Purse

'Do you think we shall get to the Tolmên before the sun gets up?' asked the little voice anxiously.

'I don't know,' Gerna answered in a low, weary voice. 'The moon is up, I think—all there is left of it, I mean—and I can see another light shining somewhere away in the east.'

'It must be later than I thought,' said the wee voice, and the little creature within the bag began to tremble with apprehension. '*Do* make haste, dear little maid! It would be quite too dreadful to be too late after all you have done to free me from Hager's power.'

'I am *awfully* tired,' was the child's answer. 'If I could only rest a few minutes I could go faster afterwards. Shall I? I am ready to drop.'

'You must not sit down until you have reached the Tolmên. I am certain the Spriggans are following in our wake. They are throwing their Thunder-axes* over every moving thing they can see, and over every motionless thing they can touch, and if they should happen to knock against you and throw one over you, they have power to keep you helpless to move until the sun has risen.'

'Why didn't they do that when I was in danger of being drowned?' asked Gerna.

'The Thunder-axes are no good except just before the rising of the sun, or the Spriggans would not be following us to use them now. You won't give up now, whatever it costs, will you, dear?'

* A stone or metal instrument found in tin-mines, and in barrows of the ancient Celts.

'Not if I can help it,' said the child wearily.

She kept going on until she reached higher ground, where she saw standing out in the semi-darkness of the early morning a great Tolmên on the brow of the moor, and over it hanging like a hunter's horn the silver curve of the old moon.

A cry of gladness broke from Gerna's lips as she saw it, which must have made all the bad little fairies, if any were about, slink away in dismay, and the sight so cheered her that her weariness left her for a time, and she sped on like a hare until she dropped down by the big stone's side.

'She saw standing out in the semi-darkness a great Tolmên.'

'We have reached the Tolmên, have we not?' asked the little voice, all a-tremble with joy.

'Yes,' panted the child; 'and the sun isn't up. I am awful glad—aren't you?'

'More glad than I dare say, dear little maid. But I am not out of prison yet. Is there any hint of the sunrise?'

'There is a pinky light over one of the Tors,' answered Gerna.

'Ah! then you must pass me through the Tolmên's hole at once. *Three times, remember*,' as Gerna put her hand in the bosom of her frock and drew out the tiny bag.

The brambles had grown up around the gray stone's hole, and almost blocked the way to it, and it was minutes before she could tear them aside and get into the opening; but she did so at last, and passed the prison-bag three times through the hole as she was bidden. As she did so, the sky in the east grew brighter and brighter, and she knew from that sign that the sun was about to rise.

'Now place the prison and me, its prisoner, on the top of the Tolmên,' cried the little voice—'longways to the east it must lie; and when you have done that, stand by the Holed Stone very quietly, then wait and see what will happen.'

Gerna did as she was told, and stood on a high bank of fragrant thyme at the head of the hoary old granite stone, with its great hole, her face towards the sunrising.

She herself was very quiet, as was also the little prisoner, but all the great wild moor was now full of music. The linnets were already twittering in the bushes, and many larks were high in the sky, singing to greet another dawn. As they sang, the east grew more and more beautiful, and behind the great Tors the sky was a wonderful rose on a background of delicate gold.

Gerna thought the sun would never show himself, and she was too tired to appreciate all the wonder of the sunrise, though she was glad enough to hear the birds singing, for it made her feel she was not so very far from home, after all.

At last the sun, red-gold and very large, wheeled up behind the shoulder of a Tor and flung out a great lance of flame across the moorland, which smote the small ring-marked purse lying on the Tolmên.

Gerna, whose gaze was now riveted on the purse, saw its ends open like a gasping fish, and then shrivel up, and in its black ashes sat the most beautiful little creature it was possible to conceive. She was so lovely and so dainty that the child could only stare at her open-mouthed with wonder and amazement.

' How can I ever thank you, dear little Gerna, for all you have done for me !' said the radiant creature, looking up into the child's amazed eyes. ' All the Wee Folks' treasures will not be deemed reward enough for the child who preferred to be compassionate than to be made rich with fairies' gold. I should not be sitting here free from *that*,' pointing to the shrivelled-up blackness which was once a Spriggan's prison, 'but for you, dear. Are you not glad you are the means of setting me free and bringing me unspeakable happiness?'

'Iss,' said Gerna, hardly knowing what she was saying, her eyes still drinking in the beauty of the little fairy. 'Aw!' she exclaimed, 'you are a dear little lovely, sure 'nough—better than all the Small People's golden pieces. You don't look a bit old, nuther.'

'You thought I should look as old as your Great-Grannie, didn't you?' laughed the happy little creature. 'The Small People show their age by looking younger and fairer—at least, the royal fairies do.'

She got on her feet as she spoke, and gazed over the great moor, and as she gazed, her face, which had the delicate pink of a cowry-shell, grew more beautiful, and a tender, happy light crept into her speedwell-blue eyes.

'There is a friend of yours crossing the moor,' she said in her sweet voice, which was more than ever like the note of a bird, only sweeter and clearer.

'Why, 'tis Farmer Vivian!' cried the child. 'However did *he* get here? I do hope he won't want to have you,' glancing at her lovely little friend anxiously. 'I don't know what I shall do to hide 'ee if he should. I couldn't put beautiful little *you* in my underskirt pocket or into the bosom of my frock.'

'Why not?' asked the dainty little creature,

smiling. ' I lay there close to your heart all this night, and a warmer, truer little heart I shall never rest against. But you need not fear Farmer Vivian on my account. He, of all persons, would not hurt any of the Good Small People for a king's crown, much less me.'

' He is getting *smaller!*' exclaimed Gerna. ' Why, he is a teeny, tiny Farmer Vivian now! Ah, dear! how queer everything is! Everything is queer an' funny since I picked up that purse with the rings 'pon it an' dear little you inside.'

' Cannot you guess who he is?' asked the little fairy, her lovely wee face more tender than the June sky over them.

' No,' returned the wondering child. ' Who is he?'

' My own little True Love!' answered the fairy, her eyes a blue light. ' We are meeting each other after a century of black years. He was my True Love all the time in the form of big Farmer Vivian! For love of poor little me he kept in the neighbourhood of Piskey Goog all that time.'

. It was all so surprising that Gerna told herself she would never be surprised any more whatever happened. And when the two Wee Lovers, separated by cruel Fate for one hundred years, met and greeted each other in lover fashion, all over the great moor broke the sound of pealing bells, so tiny and so silvery and with such music in their tones the like of which Gerna had never in all her life heard before. And where the bells were rung from she never knew, for there were no steeples or towers anywhere that she could see. As the bells' music rang on, and all the little moorland birds sang more entrancingly than before, she saw hundreds and hundreds of the Small People, all more or less beautiful, come out from behind clumps of Bog-myrtle, and banks of thyme, and beds of sweet-scented orchis,* all laughing and singing as they came towards the Tolmên, where the dear Little Lady and her True Love were standing hand in hand, smiling and bowing and looking as happy as ever they could look.

The little prisoner, who was now a prisoner no longer, seemed to be a very great personage indeed, the child thought, judging by the way the Wee Men took off their caps and bowed to her, and the little ladies made their curtseys; and in truth she was a real Princess, the eldest daughter of the King and Queen of the Good Little People, as Gerna was soon to learn.

There was great rejoicing when the Wee Folk heard how their Princess Royal had been set free, and how much Gerna had done towards it. They could not make enough of her, or do enough for her. They kissed her hands, as if she too were a Royal Princess, instead of being only a poor little Cornish peasant girl! They brought her fairy mead —*methéglin* they called it—in cups so small yet so exquisite ('like Cornish diamonds, only more lovely,' Gerna said), and gave her food to eat from dishes all iris-hued like the shells that she had picked up on

* *Gymnadénia conópæa.*

The Piskey-Purse

the sands in her own bay, only the Small People's dishes were much thinner and more transparent than any shells she had ever seen.

She was never 'treated so handsome before,' she told herself—scores and scores of dear wee creatures to wait on her and to give her more when she wanted!

When she could not eat 'a morsel more,' nor drink another cup of the all-sweet mead, her own Little Lady and her True Love, who had been sitting close to her all this time on a bed of yellow trefoil, rose up and took her through a rock-door behind the Tolmên and down into a most beautiful place — much more beautiful than she could ever have pictured in her wildest dreams.

It was the country where the Good Little People lived, 'Farmer Vivian' told her. She saw so much that she could take in nothing until they came to the King's Palace, which was the most beautiful palace in fairyland. Here she was taken into room after room—each more beautiful than the last—until she came to a place called the 'Room of the Chair,' which was full of soft voices, fragrant smells, and sweet music. This room was open to the blue dome of the sky, and away at the end of it, on a Chair, sat two Wee People with eyes the colour of her dear Little Lady's. They were not different from the other Small People surrounding the Chair, save that they had 'things on their heads,' as Gerna expressed it (which, of course, were crowns), that shone like the blue of the sea when the sun shines on it, and that they looked even more gracious and more gentle and kind than did her own Little Dear.

When the King and Queen of the Good Little People had lovingly welcomed back their long-lost daughter, and complimented their child's betrothed —who was also a very great personage in the Small People's Kingdom—for his constancy and fidelity to their dear daughter, Gerna, in her print sunbonnet and sun-faded tinker-blue frock, was introduced to their gracious Majesties as the dear little Cornish maid who preferred to be kind rather than be made rich with the Small People's gold.

Pages could be filled with what the King and Queen said to the child, who never felt so uncomfortable in her life as when they thanked her and praised her for all she had done.

'I haven't done nothing much—nothing worth a thank'ee, I mean,' she kept saying.

'Thou hast done more than thou wilt ever know,' said his tiny Majesty solemnly, ' and we feel we can never repay thee. We could, of course, reward thee with more gold than the Spriggans offered, but we are glad to know thou would'st not value it if we gave it thee. But as we are anxious to show we are not ungrateful, we will give thee the greatest of all gifts—the eye to see all that is good and beautiful in human hearts, and the power to bring it out, which alone will make thee greatly beloved. We will also teach thee to love the lowly grass as we ourselves love it, and the humble herbs, and all the gentle flowers, which make all the common roadways, moors and downs, so fragrant and beautiful. We will reveal to thee all their charms, virtues, and healing properties, so that Gerna, the maid of Polzeath, may be a blessing to her parish. And, moreover, the Good Small People shall love thee as they have never loved a human being before—not only for the sake of our beloved child, the Princess Royal of all the Good Little People, but because thou art kind and good and could not be induced to do an unkind deed even for a purseful of the Spriggans gold.'

Gerna had but dim recollections of what followed afterwards: she only knew she was led in great state by 'Dinky Farmer Vivian' on the one side, and her Wee Lady on the other, down a long lane of bowing and curtseying Little Grandees, until she came out into gardens ablaze with flowers. She was then taken through parks, where teeny, tiny deer and cows were grazing, on and on until they came to a tiny door in a cliff, when she felt the soft pressure of kisses on her face and heard the sweet wee voice she knew so well whispering in her ear, 'Good-bye, dear little maid, until we meet again—which shall be soon!' and the next moment she found herself back in Great-Grannie's poor little chamber in her own small bed, and Great-Grannie herself telling her to get up and go down to the bay 'to once' to pick limpets for the ducklings, which were nearly quacking the house down for want of their breakfast.

The Piskey-Purse

Gerna wondered as she dressed if all that had taken place that night was a dream, and she searched for the ring-marked Piskey-purse to be quite sure it wasn't. As it was nowhere to be found, nor the wee Shoes, nor the dinky Lantern, she came to the conclusion that it *must* be true.

In passing Piskey Goog on her way back from her limpet-picking, she saw a wee Brown Man with a laugh all over his merry little face, which made it delightful to look at. He took off his cap as polite as could be, and spoke to the child with the greatest respect.

'I am a *real* Piskey,' he said, introducing himself, 'and Farmer Vivian told me it would interest you to know that the Spriggans who lived in this goog were taken prisoners soon after their captive was set free, and that they were at once taken before the Gorsedd (the Little People's judgment-seat), and were tried and condemned to break iron with wooden hammers in a dark cave until they repent, which I am afraid they never will, for they are past all good feeling, poor things, and will gradually grow smaller and smaller until they turn into emmets, as all evil-minded fairies in the Small People's country do.'

'Aw dear! What a terrible punishment!' exclaimed Gerna.

'I must go back into our cavern,' said the Piskey. 'It was always ours until the Spriggans turned us out about a year ago. They can never turn us out any more now, our King says, *thanks to a little*

The Piskey-Purse

Cornish maid, who would rather be good than be rich.
We are ordered to play no pranks on the people of
this parish for her sake, even if they don't turn their
coats or stockings inside out, nor to ride any horses
in the happy night-time, except the horses of those
who have an inordinate love of money.'

And the Little Man, who was a real Piskey, went
off laughing and disappeared into Piskey Goog.

*   *   *   *   *

Years passed on. Great-Grannie died, and Gerna
grew into womanhood. She was the best-loved
person in St. Minver parish, as the King of the
Good Little People said she would be. Everybody
loved her dearly ; they loved her because she saw the
good that was in their hearts, and was not slow to
tell them of it, and because of her good opinion of
them, which although they did not always deserve,
they tried their hardest to live up to. They came to
her with their heart-wounds as well as the wounds
of their bodies, and she, who had the gift of healing
with the herbs and flowers of the earth, somehow
knew how to salve the sores of the heart too.

Gerna never grew rich, and never wanted to, and
as she would not take a penny piece or anything
greater, she had always plenty of patients. People
came to her from far as well as near, and brought,
not only themselves, but their poor suffering animals.
If the truth be told, she had a deeper compassion for
the dumb beasts, who could not tell out their
sorrows, than she had for their masters, which is

saying a great deal, and she always applied her most soothing and healing ointments to their bodies.

It was said that Gerna often saw her Little Lady and her True Love, and that the dear Wee Folk flocked to see her when the moon was up ; that they were most kind to her, and even brought her herbs and flowers, wet with fairy dew, for her simples, and helped her to make eye-salves and other healing things, which the poor people declared 'made them such a power for good.'

It was also told that the merry little Piskey Men danced on the top of Pentire Glaze cliffs for her special amusement, and that when they knew she was watching them, their laughter rang out clear as bells across the Polzeath beach of grey, gold sand.

The Magic Pail

O N a lonely moor lying between Carn Kenidzhek*
and Bosvavas Carn lived one Tom Trebisken
and Joan his wife. They had been married
up in the teens of years, and had no child, which was
a disappointment to
them both, especially
to Joan, who suffered
from rheumatism,
which had crip-
pled her feet.

Tom had long
given up all hope of
having a child, but
Joan still believed that
one would come to
them some day, and
it cheered her dreary
hours, as she sat helpless
in her armchair, to think
of the advent of the little
one, who would gladden
their life. Every six days in seven she spent abso-

A Cornish Tin-mine.

* Pronounced Kenidjack.

59

lutely alone, for Tom worked as surface-man all the year round at Ding Dong, a great tin-mine, or bal, at the other end of their moor, and had to leave for his work early in the morning, and did not return until late in the evening; so it was not surprising that she wanted a child, and that she sometimes cried in her heart: 'Aw that I had a little maid of my own to do things for me an' keep me company when my Tom is away all day at the bal !'

The part of the moor where the Trebiskens lived was three miles or more from Ding Dong, and two miles from their nearest neighbour. It was quite out of the beaten track, and a passer by their cottage was as rare as blackberries in December. They would not have lived there at all, but that the cottage was their own—or, rather, Joan's. It had been left to her by will, with the condition that they should live in it themselves.

The cottage was not an ordinary one; its walls were built of small blocks of mica and porphyry— much of the porphyry being of that lovely deep-pink kind, with blotchings of black hornblende, all of which a long century or more of weather had polished to the smoothness of glass. Joan said the weather had nothing whatever to do with it, and that it was done by the dear Little People* who, she declared, lived in the carn near where the cottage stood. But whoever polished the walls—weather or fairies—the house was a pleasure to look at, particu-

* Fairies.

The Magic Pail

larly when the sun began to sink behind the moors
and shone full upon its walls; for then all the richness of the porphyry's rose, all the hornblende's soft
blackness, and all the mica's brilliancy, were brought
out of the stone, and intensified until a less imagi-
native person than Joan Trebisken would have
believed it was built by enchantment. Even its
commonplace roof of brown thatch, which over-
spread the small casement windows in shaggy
raggedness, did not take from the burning wonder of
the walls. Perhaps it was because a company of stone-
crop had found a dwelling-place there, and that on the
ridge of the roof stood out in red distinctness half a
dozen *Pysgy-pows**—curious little round-knobbed
tiles placed there by Joan's forebears for the Piskeys
to dance on.

Joan, poor soul, seldom saw the outside splendour
of their cottage, as she was powerless to move from
her chair without help, and when her Tom came home,
his face was the only thing she wanted to see, she
said. Fortunately, however, her doors and windows
opened on to the moor, and she could therefore
command from where she sat a long stretch of moorland, which, though wild, was none the less beautiful
at every season of the year, but especially in the
springtime, when the yellow broom and golden
gorse were in flower.

In spite of its loneliness, Joan loved the moor with

* Ridge-tiles with knobs, which people in West Cornwall put
on their houses for the Piskeys to dance on.

all her Celtic nature, and spent most of her day looking out upon it until the days shortened and *Nisdhu,*
the Black Month, which the Cornish of our time call
November, drew near.

Nobody dreaded that dark month, with its damp
clinging cold, its fogs and mists, which often veiled
the whole landscape, including the great carns, more
than Joan. She said she felt the chill of its breath
before it showed its nose over the head of Carn
Kenidzhek, and was careful to shut her door and
hatch and her small casement-windows before
October was half through. She was sorry to do this,
and would not have done so but for the pain in her
bones, which was always worse when November was
on its way; for she shut out, she said, the music of
the Small People's voices.

Tom told her it wasn't the voices of the Wee Folk
she heard, but the trickling of a little stream making
its way down by the carn on its way across the moor.
But she declared she knew better, and had ears to
distinguish between the tinkle of water and the
sweet voices of the dear Little People, if he had not,
and Tom, like a sensible man, let her hold to her
belief.

Joan was a great believer in the fairies, and often
declared they were very friendly towards her—
perhaps because her forebears had put the pysgy-pows
on the roof of their cottage for them to dance on. It
was her regret that she had never seen any of the
dear little creatures; but she lived in hope of seeing

The Magic Pail

them some day; perhaps when the much-cried-for little maid came she should see them then, she said.

It was now towards the end of October and exceedingly cold, and her door and window being shut, she felt very wisht;* and as the days jogged on to dreary November she became terribly depressed, so much so that Tom dreaded to leave her sitting all alone by the chimney-corner with a face as long as a fiddle.

He was one of the kindest husbands in the world, and never went to his work without doing all that lay in his power to make her comfortable while he was away. She was generally very appreciative and grateful for all he did for her; but to-day—the day on which something happened to alter the whole circumstances of her life—she grumbled at everything he did, even when he piled dry peat and furze within her reach, filled the kettle and put it on the brandis,† and placed her dinner on a small table by her side. She would not even look at him, or say good-bye, when at last he had to go off to the mine in the dark of the autumnal morning, which made her feel more sad than ever when he was out of her sight.

A fog of depression hung over her spirits all that long day, and the weather, as if to share her gloom, was foggy too. She could not see a yard beyond her window most of the day; and when the mist did lift for a little while, it took such fantastic

* Sad.   † An iron stool.

forms she was glad when it again hung down like a curtain.

When the hour for Tom's return at last drew near she grew more cheerful. She put on the last of the furze he had placed within reach of her hand, partly to boil the kettle and to light him down the road leading to their cottage, but chiefly to make her kitchen cheery-looking to make up for his cold send-off.

She was on the watch now for his step, and her face grew brighter as she listened. The kettle was crooning on the fire and everything was warm in cheerful welcome as a step was heard on the hard road outside, and a hand fumbled at the door-latch.

Joan, being all impatience to see her man, cried out :

' What are 'ee so stupid about, an ? Give the door a shove, soas !* 'Tis sticked by the damp.'

She had scarcely said this when the door and its hatch opened gently, and in the doorway stood—not her husband, as she supposed, but the bent figure of a tiny old woman with a small costan, or bramble-basket, on her back. Her slight form was enveloped in a cloak the colour of far-away hills, and her face hidden in the depths of a large bonnet, such as the mine-maidens wear at their work in the mines.

Joan was too amazed to see a stranger at her door to ask what she wanted, and before she could get over her surprise, the little old woman had come into

* A coaxing expression, such as ' Do ee dear.'

The Magic Pail

the cottage, stepped noiselessly to the hearthplace,
unslung the costan, and laid it at her feet, singing
as she did so a curious rhyme in a voice so wild and

*' A tiny old woman with a small costan, or bramble-basket, on
her back.'*

sweet, it reminded Joan, as she listened, which she
did as one in a dream, of moor-birds' music and
rippling streams, and the voices of the Small People

5

who lived among the carns. The rhyme was as follows :

> ' I bring thee and leave thee my little mudgeskerry !*
> My dinky,† my dear !
> Till the day of that year
> When the spells shall be broken—
> And this is the token—
> By Magic and Pail
> And the Skavarnak's ‡ wail,
> My ninnie, my dinnie, my little mudgeskerry !

> ' Then we to the carns will away, my pednpaley §
> My deary, my tweet !
> Where the Small People's feet
> Tread out the Birth measure,
> To give *her* a treasure
> From out of the blue,
> When she shall know too
> 'Tis better to give than to keep my pednpaley.'

The song and its music had hardly died away, when the tiny old woman spread her hands over the bramble-basket, as if in blessing, and then stole out of the cottage as noiselessly and mysteriously as she had come.

Joan was all of a tremble quite five minutes

---

* Mudgeskerry, or skerrymudge, anything grotesque in human shape, such as a doll.

† Dinky, *very* small.

‡ Skavarnak, long-eared ; also a hare.

§ Pednpaley, a blue-tit ; also anything very soft and beautiful, such as velvet. Literally, *a soft-head*. The ' d ' in this word is silent.

after she had gone, and when she had somewhat recovered herself, her glance fell on the costan. At first she was afraid what it contained; but her woman's curiosity got the better of her fears, and, bending over the rough basket, she turned over the bracken, laid in careful order on its top, and saw lying on a bed of dried moss and leaves something that brought a cry of amazement, mingled with horror, to her lips.

It was a babe, but so tiny and so ugly that she shuddered as she gazed upon it. It was in a deep sleep, or seemed to be, and its skinny little face, crinkled all over like a poppy just out of its sheath, was resting on its claw-like hand.

In all her dreams of a child coming to her home, Joan had never dreamt of anything so uncanny as this babe, and she told herself that the little creature in its costan cradle was sent to punish her for her persistent desire for a child.

Tom arrived just then, and soon knew all that his wife could tell of the mysterious coming and going of the little old woman in the bal-bonnet, and of her strange song; and, like Joan, when he looked into the bramble-basket and saw the bit of ugliness within, he gave voice to a cry of horror that anything so uncanny should be left on their hands. In fact, he was so angry that he wanted to take the basket and all it held on to the moor, and let her who brought it come and take it away, for have it in his house he would not—no, not for all the crocks of gold the Little People were said to have in their keeping.

The night was bitterly cold, and by little moans and sighs coming from the direction of the Hooting Carn Joan could tell the wind was about to rise, and would perhaps end in a great storm. And though she was so much upset at having such an ugly little creature thrust on them, she was too tender-hearted to wish it to be exposed even for an hour on their moor on such a night. Besides, the child was helpless, whosoever child it was, and therefore demanded compassion, and she begged her husband to allow it to stay in their house until to-morrow.

Tom could seldom refuse his crippled wife anything when her heart was set upon it, and, though much against his inclination, he yielded to her entreaties; but he was careful to add that he could only suffer it to stay until he was ready to start for the bal.

'Whatever the weather then, fair or foul, out it shall go on the moor!' he cried. 'It is a changeling,' he added, with a solemn shake of his head, 'and if we was to let it abide along o' we, we should have nothing but bad luck all the rest of our days.'

Joan, having got her way, did not care to contradict her husband; for she told herself the song the little old woman had sung pointed to something quite different. Still, she would not keep the babe longer than the morrow if he were against it.

When bedtime came, Tom and Joan had quite a

The Magic Pail

dispute as to where the strange cradle and its stranger occupant should be put for the night, and as neither of them could decide, and Tom was against its being taken up into the bed-chamber, Joan declared she would sit up with it all night, and nothing Tom could say should prevent her. So he went off to his bed in a huff, muttering loudly that the cheeld,* or 'whatever it was,' had brought misery to them already.

Joan kept to her resolve, and sat in her armchair with the bramble-basket at her feet until well on towards the dawn, when Tom came down to see how she was faring, and found, to his surprise, she was as fresh as a rose just gathered.

'An' I ent sleepy nuther!' she cried in triumph. 'I ent felt so well since I was took with the rheumatics, and me hands don't look so twisted, do they?' holding them up. ''Tis my belief 'tis all owing to that little cheeld down there in the costan.'

As Tom could not gainsay this, he went off to do his morning's work, and to get Joan's breakfast. By the time he had done this the sun was rising, and the sky, away in the east, was a miracle of purple and rose. The night had been wild, but the storm having exhausted itself, the dawn was all the more beautiful.

The babe was still asleep, and had not moved all night, Joan said, and Tom fervently hoped it would

* Child.

69

The Magic Pail

not until it was safe out on the moor. But he hoped
in vain, for when the sun began to wheel up behind
the hills in the east, and sent a beam of rosy light in
at the casement window, the little creature shuffled
in the costan, and when Joan, willing to give it air,
pushed back its covering of bracken, it opened its eyes
and smiled, and that smile transformed its whole
face.

' Why, Tom, my man,' she cried, ' the little dear
isn't ugly one bit ; an' the little eyes of it are as soft
as moor-pools ! Do 'ee come and have a squint at it.'

Tom came, and when he had stared at the babe a
minute or more, he said slowly, as if weighing his
words :

' You be right, Joan ; but it do make the mystery
all the more queer. A cheeld that can look as ugly
as nettles one minute and as pretty as flowers the
next ent for *we* to keep.'

' Dont 'ee betray thy ignorance where babes is
concerned !' cried Joan, fearful of what his words
implied. ' Some do look terrible plain in their
sleep—as this poor dear did—and some do look
beautiful. 'Tis as Nature made 'em—bless their
hearts !'

The babe now turned her eyes on Tom, and was
gazing on him as if she wanted to look into his very
soul, and then, as if she quite approved of what she
saw there, gave him a fascinating smile, which won
his heart at once.

' You won't take the cheeld out on the moors

to-day, Tom, will 'ee?' asked Joan, who was quick to see the change in her man's face.

'We will keep it till I come home from the bal, at any rate,' he said cautiously. And then the babe, as if to show its gratitude for the concession, held up both its little arms to him to be taken out of its costan cradle, whereupon Tom was so delighted at being preferred before his wife that he could hardly conceal his pride.

'That infant do knaw a thing or two, whatever it be,' said Joan to herself, with a chuckle. 'And 'tis a *somebody*, I can tell, by her little shift and things, which do look as if they was spun out of spiders' webs by the Small People, so fine an' silky they be !'

There was no question now about the little stranger staying ; but, all the same, Tom went off to the mine with many misgivings, and he said to himself, as he walked quickly over the moor, that if Joan were too helpless to do for herself, how was she going to tend a babe ? And that thought troubled him all the day.

But his fears were needless ; for when he got home that evening and looked in at the door, he saw a sight which surprised him, yet gladdened his heart. Joan was sitting in her elbow-chair, with a face as bright as a moon in a cloudless sky, cuddling the strange babe, who was babbling to the kind face looking down into it as it lay in her arms.

'However did 'ee manage to lift the cheeld on to your lap, Joan ?' he asked, when his wife saw him.

'Aw ! we managed somehow or tuther between us,'

she answered, with a happy laugh. 'It was as light as a feather, it was,' chirping to the babe, 'an' I do think the Small People gave it a hoist on to Mammie Trebisken's lap! Eh, my handsome?' speaking to the babe. 'An' it haven't a been a mite o' trouble nuther all this blessed day!' And then, looking up at Tom with a look he never forgot: 'An' it have a-lifted the latch of my loneliness, an' I am as happy as a queen!'

Tom was thankful to hear all this, and he thought it was no accident that had brought such comfort to his poor lonely wife. He had still greater cause for thankfulness as the days wore on; for as Joan now had her thoughts taken from herself in having a babe—which, by the way, was a maiden babe—to think for and to attend to as far as she was able, she grew better in health, and before winter was over could go about the house-place 'and do all her little chores her own self,' she proudly declared. She even swept and sanded her kitchen floor, and made figgy hoggans* for her husband's dinner, which she had not been able to do since the early years of their marriage.

There were, however, a few things Joan could not do; but as they were all done for her in some mysterious way, and much better than she herself could have done, it was more a matter for rejoicing than regret. Whenever she put her washing out in the backlet † to wait till Tom had time to do it,

* Miners' pasties.   † Back-kitchen.

' " *However did 'ee manage to lift the cheeld on to your lap?* " '

somebody took it away, and brought it back washed and dried and ironed—all looking as white as Mayblossom and smelling as sweet as moor-flowers!

She was never certain who did this kindness for her, but in her heart she believed it was either done by the little old woman who brought the babe or the Small People.

Several happy years passed away, and the little child—*Ninnie-Dinnie*, as they called her—so strangely brought to the moorland cottage and so strangely left, was now able to return some of her foster-parents' kindness. This she did by helping in small household duties.

Joan, partly because it was right and partly because she feared the rheumatism might some day make her helpless again, had brought her up to be useful.

The child did not at all like work, and, but for Joan's insistence, would have been a regular little do-nothing. Perhaps she would have spared the little maid from many a small household duty if the Pail had allowed it!

In shaking up the moss and leaves in the bramble-basket the evening the mysterious little woman brought it to the cottage, Tom had found at the feet of the babe a small dark Pail, which he said must have been shaped out of a block of black tin left by the Old Men, or ancient Jews, who, ages before the art of turning black tin into white was discovered, worked the Cornish tin-mines. It was very crude,

The Magic Pail

and had nothing remarkable about it save for its look of age and some curious characters cut under its rim, and which, of course, neither he nor his wife could read.

They thought the Pail was put into the bramble-basket for the child to play with, and telling themselves they would give her a better plaything when she was old enough, they set it on the dresser.

They were soon to learn that the Pail was something more than a child's toy, and had strange properties of making itself light or dark at will, thrusting its characters out of the metal in strong relief from its surface and withdrawing them again!

Tom declared it had in some mysterious way to do with the little creature's welfare, and that it was a kind of conscience—a Small People's conscience, perhaps. But Joan said she believed it was something more than that, if there was any meaning in the words of the song the dinky old woman in the bal-bonnet had sung.

But, whoever was right, there was no doubt that the Pail showed its approval or disapproval of whatever Ninnie-Dinnie did! If the little maid was especially helpful and kind, the Pail became a lovely shade of silver and gray, and its letters stood out in glittering distinctness; but if she was lazy, or spoke rudely to her foster-parents, it grew darker than hornblende, and its characters were hardly visible.

This strange property of the Pail made Joan feel quite creepy when she first discovered its peculiarity, which she happened to do one day when Ninnie-Dinnie was very fractious and would do nothing she was bidden. She got used to it in time, and was even glad it showed its pleasure, or otherwise, in the manner it did.

She often told her husband that, when the little maid was particularly kind to her when he was at the bal, the Pail would laugh all over its sides.

Ninnie-Dinnie was now in her eighth year, counting the year she was brought to the cottage, and a dear, useful little maid she was ; and no one to beat her anywhere for work, Tom declared, particularly when her size was considered.

The child was very small, so small that she could still sleep in the basket cradle she came in—and did too, for the simple reason that she was wakeful all night if she slept anywhere else.

Both Tom and Joan were sometimes troubled at her size. For she never seemed to grow bigger or fatter, whatever they gave her to eat, and they feared she would always be a little Go-by-the-ground.* Joan, however, consoled herself that perhaps she was an off relation of the dear Little People.

Although Ninnie-Dinnie was exceedingly tiny, she was very sharp, and asked more questions in a day than they could answer in a year. She wanted to know the why and wherefore of everything—what the moor-flowers were made of, and who lived inside the great grey carns, and what made Carn Kenidzhek

* A *very* short person.

hoot—was it the giant who lived inside it?—and much besides that neither Tom nor Joan could answer, because they did not know themselves.

Tom said she was wise beyond her years, and all owing to her being moped in the cottage so much, and that she ought to be out of doors more. Joan quite agreed with him, and suggested that he should take her with him sometimes over the moor, only stipulating that she was not to go as far as the mine-works.

Tom considered this a splendid idea; and so, every now and then, when Ninnie-Dinnie was willing, she accompanied him part of the way, and as there was only one road leading back to the cottage, she easily found her way home alone.

One day, when the child had reached the place where the miner generally sent her back, she begged to go with him all the way to the bal; and as he was rather weak where his womenfolk were concerned, he willingly consented.

When they reached Ding Dong, with its hundreds of busy workers, the little maid grew very frightened, and fled back across the moor, in the direction of home, as fast as her legs could take her.

The miner, as he watched her running away, rather reproached himself for bringing her so far; and he wondered, as he put the tin into the furnace to be smelted, whether she got home all right.

'So you *did* take our Ninnie-Dinnie to the bal?' was his wife's greeting when he got home that

The Magic Pail

evening. ' I've been terribly wisht* without her all day.'

' You don't mean to say the little dear haven't come back ?' cried Tom. ' That is terrible news, sure 'nough ! She didn't stop a minute at the bal, and tore off home like a skainer.'†

' I've never clapt eyes on her since she went out with 'ee this morning !' cried Joan, greatly distressed. ' I do hope nothing has happened to her. Perhaps she has been an' gone an' tumbled down into one of the Old Men's workings ‡ out there on the moor.'

Tom went as white as a sheet at the bare thought of the possibility, and he started off at once to look for the child, leaving his poor wife more troubled than she had ever been since Ninnie-Dinnie came.

He was gone a little over an hour, when, to Joan's thankfulness, he returned with the child.

He found her, he said, not far from the beaten track, sitting at the foot of a carn waiting for him to come for her.

She told him she had lost her way, and that as she was sitting on the griglans,§ an ugly little man with long ears like a Skavarnak‖ came up to her, and because she was afraid of him and would not go into his little house under the carn, he was very angry. She did not know what would have happened to her if a little old woman in a sunbonnet had not come along just then, and took her to the place

---

* Lonely.   † One who runs very fast.   ‡ Disused mines.
§ Heath.   ‖ A hare.

The Magic Pail

where Tom found her. She told her to sit where she was till Daddie Trebisken came to fetch her, which he would be sure to do after sunset. In the meantime she was to say her own name backwards seven times if the Long-Eared came near her again. She also told her that Ninnie-Dinnie, if she cared to believe it, was her real name spelt backwards with an 'n' left out; and she said she must never go out on the lonely moors without taking the Pail, made out of old Cornish tin, with her.

It was ever so long before Joan got over her fright about Ninnie-Dinnie, and for weeks she would not hear of her going out on the moors. But, as time deadens all things, she got over her nervousness, and when April came, and the broom and the gorse were in flower, making the great brown moor yellow-gold, and scenting all the air with peach-like fragrance, she was willing that the little maid should go with her husband once more. And Tom willingly took her.

As they were going out of the door, something fell on the Pail standing on the dresser, and the child, remembering the injunction of the little old woman about the Pail, turned back to get it.

'What shall I bring 'ee home, Mammie Trebisken?' she asked, looking at her foster-mother; and Joan, hearing the lark singing faintly in the distance, replied laughingly:

'You shall bring me home a pailful of lark's music, my dear.'

'You do knaw the little maid can't bring 'ee *that*,'

cried Tom impatiently. ' I should think *she* was all the music you wanted now.'

' So she is, bless her !' said his wife. ' I was only joking.'

' Nevertheless, I will bring you home this Pail full of lark's music,' said Ninnie-Dinnie, with great seriousness ; and putting her tiny hand into Tom's big one, they started off, and Joan watched them out of sight.

When the miner and the child got about half-way to the mine, scores of larks were up in the blue air singing, and their little dark bodies waving to and fro in the rapture of their song, till it seemed to the miner as if their melody was trickling down all over him, and Ninnie-Dinnie declared it *was*.

As they stood listening, one of the larks began to descend, singing as it came.

' Now is the time if you want to catch the lark's music for Mammie Trebisken,' laughed Tom, watching the bird's descent. ' There it is, just over thy soft little head. Up with thy Pail, my dear !'

And Ninnie-Dinnie, with her face as grave as the great boulders lying amongst the golden-blossomed furze and the feathery fronds of the Osmunda, lifted the Pail above her head, and as she did so the strange letters under its rim stood out and glowed like white fire.

' Little lark, little lark, give me thy music !' she chanted in a voice as clear and sweet as linnets'

The Magic Pail

fluting. 'Little lark, little lark, give me thy song!' and the small bird twirled down towards her singing wilder and sweeter as it came, until it hovered over the uplifted Pail.

It hovered over the uplifted Pail.'

'The dear little lark has given me its music and its song to make Mammie Trebisken's heart glad,' said the child, as the lark dropped on the thyme-scented turf at her feet.

'Pretending, are 'ee, an?' laughed Tom.

'*No!*' cried Ninnie-Dinnie. 'Listen!'

And the miner, putting his ear close to the Pail, heard, to his unspeakable amazement, a lark singing quite distinctly, yet rather faintly, as it were singing far away.

'Jimmerychry!* Can it be believed?' he exclaimed. ''Tis magic, an' I don't half like it. An' I don't think the dear little bird do nuther,' looking down at the lark, who was trailing its wings on the

* A note of exclamation.

The Magic Pail

ground in that distressful way birds have when their wee nestlings are in danger. 'Give it back its own, that's a dear little maid.'

'I can't,' said Ninnie-Dinnie. 'Mammie Trebisken can only do that; and I don't think she will want to, for the song in the Pail will make all her heart sing.'

She covered the Pail with her pinafore as she spoke, and the little lark disappeared into a brake of flaming gorse.

There was no time to bandy words, Tom told himself, as he was late for his work, and he left the child to go back to their cottage without any more protesting. But he did not feel very comfortable as he strode on his way to the mine.

It was late in the morning when Ninnie-Dinnie got home, and Joan was beginning to be troubled at her long absence when she came in.

'Have 'ee brought the lark's music along with 'ee?' she asked, as the child set the Pail on the red-painted dresser.

'Yes,' said Ninnie-Dinnie; 'and at sundown you will hear it.'

Joan, thinking it was all make-believe, laughed, and said she would keep her ears open to listen.

When the shadows of the great grey carns stretched over the heather and the sun sunk over the moor, the Pail began to move slightly on the dresser, and a sound came out like grass moved gently by the wind, which at once drew Joan's attention to it. Then, to her amazement, it shook all over, and there poured forth from it such a gush of melody that almost took her breath away. It was like lark's music, she said, with a strain of sweeter, wilder music added to it, and which, somehow, reminded her of the flute-like voice of the little old woman in the bal-bonnet, who sang that rude rhyme when she brought them their dear little Ninnie-Dinnie. She sat in her elbow-chair entranced, and the queer child sat at her feet, apparently entranced too!

The melody, which at first came from the depths of the Pail, or the turfy ground, it was hard to say which, rose higher and higher, until it sounded like a bird singing its heart out in the soft azure of an evening sky.

Joan never knew how long she listened to that fetterless song; she only knew she awoke to the fact that the sky's little songster, the Pail, or whatever it was, had stopped singing, that daylight was leaving the moor, and that a small dark shadow was slowly stealing across her window.

'Why, it is a little bird, surely,' she said, speaking to the tiny maid at her feet. 'The light of our fire have attracted it from its sleeping-place—poor little thing!'

'P'r'aps it is the little lark come for its music and its song,' suggested Ninnie-Dinnie, fixing her gaze on the bird, which was now fluttering against the panes and uttering a tiny note of distress.

The Magic Pail

'I never thought of that,' said Joan. 'I hope it haven't. I couldn't give it back its song and its music for the world!'

As she was speaking, the Pail on the dresser was again agitated, and out of it rushed another entrancing melody, until all the cottage was full of music, and Joan said it was raining down upon her head from the oaken beams. But through the melody could be distinctly heard a little voice, which was the lark's voice :

'Give me back my music! Give me back my song !'

'My Aunt Betsy!' cried Joan. 'Whoever heard of a bird talking before ?'

'Are you going to give the little lark what it wants?' asked Ninnie-Dinnie, watching the bird, which was still fluttering against the bottle-green pane.

'*No !*' said Joan decidedly. 'I don't think I ought. It do make my heart young an' happy again.'

'I was hoping you would like to give back the lark its music and its song,' said Ninnie-Dinnie.

'Whatever for, cheeld-vean ?'* Joan asked.

'Because,' answered the child, 'I have been wondering what the lark's little mate will do if he hasn't his song to sing to her now she is sitting on her pretty eggs out on the grass.'

'Why, make another song, of course, you foolish little knaw-nothing !' cried Joan, laying her pain-twisted fingers on the child's elfin locks.

* Little child.

85

The Magic Pail

' It has no music to make a song with; it gave it all to me to take home to my dear Mammie Trebisken,' said the little maid.

Once more the lark's song came out of the Pail, and Joan said it was sweeter and wilder and freer than even the second time. As she listened intently she was carried to her courting days, when she and Tom took their Sunday walks through the growing corn and flaming poppies to hear the larks sing. Then as the songster came earthward again and its music died away into the silence of the years, or into the Pail, she was too bewildered to say which, there appeared on the threshold of the door the little lark, which, as she looked at it, trailed its wings and piped: ' Give me back my music! Give me back my song !' and its sad cry went right down into her pitiful heart.

' I was a selfish body to want to keep what didn't belong to me,' she cried, and she told Ninnie-Dinnie to give it back what it wanted.

' I can't give back: you only can do that,' said the little maid. ' I can only bring you what you ask.'

The wee bird in the doorway again made itself heard: ' Give me back my music! Give me back my song !' and so distressful was its pleading that she clutched the child's shoulder and went at once to the dresser, and, almost before she knew it, she was standing at the door with the Pail in her hand.

' Take your music and your song, you poor little dear,' she said in her tenderest voice to the bird;

The Magic Pail

' and go along home to your mate, and make her as happy as you have made my heart this day.'

She turned the Pail over on its side as she spoke, and the lark flew into it; and in a minute or less it was out again and away into the semi-darkness, singing its own ecstatic song as it went!

Tom came up the road as it flew off; and as she waited there by the door for him to help her back to her chair, the little old woman's rhyme came back to her, the last line of which floated through her brain :

> ' To give her a treasure
> From out of the blue,
> When she shall know too
> 'Tis better to give than to keep my pednpaley !'

A year and four months went by, and Joan was quite helpless again—as helpless as when the babe was brought to her—and but for that babe, now to childhood grown, she did not know what she would have done. Her man was not so young as he was, and had a great deal more to do at the mine, and therefore less time to devote to woman's work. But thanks to Ninnie-Dinnie's careful training, his services in this respect were not required. The little maid now did all the work of the small cottage, and the cooking too—even to making the hoggans for Tom's dinner. Besides which, she waited on her dear Mammie Trebisken hand and foot, and made the poor sufferer's life as happy as possible under the circumstances. Tom wondered how she did it all,

The Magic Pail

'and such a dinky little soul too—not much bigger than a little pednpaley itself,' he said.

Ninnie-Dinnie did not go out on the moor all this time, and nothing Joan could say would make her. But when July came, and the blackberry brambles were in flower, and the great moors began to look beautifully purple with the bloom of the heather, she cast wistful glances out of the window, and one bright morning she asked Tom to take her with him a little way.

Her eye caught the darkening look of the Pail as she was putting on her sunbonnet, and she thought the look meant she must take it with her, and she did.

'What shall I bring you home?' she asked, looking over her shoulder at Joan as she and Tom were going out of the door; and the invalid, catching sight of a sunbeamed pool lying high on the heath, said, with a laugh :

'You shall bring me home a pailful of sunbeams from the pool I can see from my chair.'

'A pack of nonsense !' cried Tom. 'As well ask for the moon. I should have thought that our Ninnie-Dinnie,' resting his huge hand on the child's head, 'was all the sunbeam you wanted now.'

'So she is, Tom, when *you* ent here,' cried the woman, smiling tenderly at both her dears.

'All the same,' said Ninnie-Dinnie, 'I will bring you home a pailful of sunbeams if I can.'

When she and Tom reached the pool, they stopped

The Magic Pail

and looked in, or tried to, for they could not see its bottom for sunbeams, which rippled all over its surface in tiny waves of light.

' Now is your chance to get that pailful of sunbeams thy foolish old Mammie Trebisken axed 'ee to get,' said the miner.

' It is,' said Ninnie‑Dinnie in her grave old woman's manner; and, leaning over the pool, she held the Pail over the side and cried: ' Little brown pool, give me thy sunbeams! Little brown pool, give me thy light !' and, to Tom's amazement (he ought not to have been astonished at anything by this time), he saw the light leave the pool and flow into the Pail!

When the moor-pool had given all its sunbeams. and the water was a darker brown than a sparrow's back, Ninnie-Dinnie stood up and looked into her Pail, and Tom looked too, and saw nothing.

' It is full of emptiness,' said he, laughing.

' It is full of the dear little Pool's sunbeams to make Mammie Trebisken's eyes glad,' insisted the child; and covering the Pail very carefully with her pinafore, she went down towards the cottage, and Tom watched her until she was hidden behind a great boulder of granite, and then he too went on his way.

Ninnie-Dinnie did not get home till quite late in the afternoon, and when Joan asked her where she had been so long, she said a little Skavarnak would not let her come before, and that he stood in the path barring the way, till a dinky little woman in a bluish cloak came over the moor, and then he sped away through a hole in a carn.

'What a funny thing!' said Joan; 'hares generally keep out of folks' way. He must be different from other little hares.'

'I am sure he must be,' she said, setting the Pail on the dresser.

'Have 'ee brought the sunbeams?' asked Joan, turning her gaze to the bucket.

'Yes; and by-and-by, when the sun begins to set, you will be able to see them.'

Joan, thinking her Ninnie-Dinnie was pretending —for she saw when the child came into the kitchen that the Pail contained nothing—only laughed.

When the great round sun dropped down to his setting, the crippled woman, happening to turn her face to the dresser, saw a tongue of white flame rise out of the Pail, and on its tip burnt a ruby star!

It startled her almost out of her senses at first; but as it did not grow bigger, but only increased in beauty, she gazed at it with wondering delight.

As the evening darkened over the moor, and the Hooting Carn was dim in the distance, the light in the Pail grew exceedingly beautiful, and took all manner of shapes and colours, and made the room where Joan sat as lovely as the dear Small People's Country, Ninnie-Dinnie said—how she knew, it did not occur to her foster-mother to inquire.

The Magic Pail

' 'Tis magic !' cried the woman, looking round the room, ' an' I don't understand it one bit.'

' P'r'aps,' said the child softly, ' it is the dear Little People's way of showing how grateful they feel for your kindness to your little Ninnie-Dinnie.'

' I haven't been kinder than I ought,' began Joan ; ' and—'tis raining, surely,' she broke off, as a trickle of water fell on her ear. ' 'Tis queer, too ! There's no sign of wet weather in the sky.'

The child went to the window and looked out.

' There is a tiny stream of water coming down the road,' she said. ' I believe 'tis the little brown Pool coming for its sunbeams.'

' Don't be silly !' cried Joan.

' It *is*,' said the little maid, looking out again, ' and it has made itself into a dark ring outside our door.'

As she was speaking, a rippling voice broke out :

' Give me back my light ! give me back my sun-beams !'

' I *won't*,' said Joan irritably. ' Why should I, when it is making my little place look handsome ? I haven't seen anything like it in all my born days !'

' I was hoping you would give back the poor little brown Pool its shine,' said Ninnie-Dinnie, with a pleading look in her eyes. ' The little flowers that live in the Pool will *die* without light, and the dear little Sundews will have no silver beads to tip their red spikes.'

' Whatever did 'ee bring me home a pailful of sun-

beams for, if you want me to give it away again?'
asked the woman still more irritably.

'You *asked* me to bring you the brown Pool's sunbeams,' said the child gently. 'I did but do what
you asked.'

The light in the Pail was redder and brighter than
the red planet Mars in his rising or the sun in his
setting, and all in the room was a lovely crimson
glow, and Joan, as she gazed at the Pail again, heard
the rippling voice outside her door: 'Give me my
light! give me my sunbeams!' and it continued
rippling its demand until the woman's kind heart
was troubled.

'Poor little Pool!' she said to herself at last. 'I
expect it is feeling as wisht without its light as I was
before my Ninnie-Dinnie came in the costan. 'Tis
wrong to want to keep what will brighten something
else. I don't s'pose even a little moor-pool can be
happy and bear flowers on its bosom without sunbeams and light,' and she told the child to give back
the Pool its own.

'I *can't*,' said Ninnie-Dinnie. 'Only *you* can do
that. Lean on me,' offering her tiny arm, 'and I'll
help you to get the Pail to give the dear little Pool
its sunbeams.'

Joan was greatly amused that a dinky little maid
like her, scarcely bigger than a large doll, could
support a great helpless body like herself to walk
across the floor; and she laughed, and, as she laughed,
the Pool cried again in such a beseeching voice that

The Magic Pail

she unwittingly put her hand on the child's shoulder, and immediately found herself at the door, with the Pail in her hand, before she knew !

' I give 'ee back your brightness, dear little Pool,' she said, ' and much obliged I am to 'ee for letting me have it here in my little room. Now go along home to where you belong, amongst the griglans.'* And the little Pool took its shine and left, twisting and twirling its way back to its place, shining and rippling as it went.

' The pool will shine all the more brightly to-morrow for having given you its sunbeams,' said the child, as she helped Joan back to her chair.

A few days after Ninnie-Dinnie had brought the pailful of sunbeams, she again asked to go with Tom over the moors, and Tom willingly took her.

' What impossible thing is Mammie Trebisken going to ask you to bring back to-day ?' said the miner in joke as the child went to the dresser for the Pail.

' The only thing I should like to have brought home to me to-day is that nasty little Skavarnak which frightened my Ninnie-Dinnie,' said Joan. ' If she do catch un an' bring un home in the Pail, I won't be willing to let him get out of it again in a hurry !'

' Do you really want the Little Long-Eared ?' asked the child, with a curious look in her eyes.

' Of course I do. I s'pose he won't be so easy to

* Heath.

get into the Pail as the lark's music or the pool's sunbeams.'

'Not nearly so easy,' responded Ninnie-Dinnie. 'And even if I *can* get him into the Pail, you won't like to keep him, and you *must* until——'

She did not finish what she was going to say, as Tom was in a hurry to be off, and they left the invalid greatly wondering whatever the little maid could mean.

The sun was rising when Tom and his little foster-child reached a part of the great moor where a road turned towards Ding Dong, and where they saw a hare sitting on his haunches cleaning his whiskers.

'There is Mister Long-Eared,' whispered Tom. 'Now is your chance to catch him, my dear;' but the hare had heard the whisper, and he vanished under the bracken.

'He will be very difficult to get into the Pail,' sighed Ninnie-Dinnie. 'But he will have to go into it, or the spell won't be broken.'

'What spell?' asked the miner.

'What! have you forgotten the rhyme the dinky woman sang when she brought *me* to Mammie Tre-visken—

> 'By magic and Pail,
> And the Skavarnak's wail'?

'I had clean forgotten,' said Tom. 'But I don't s'pose it meant anything. P'r'aps the little body in the bal-bonnet didn't know what she was singing.'

The miner went on his way to Ding Dong, and

The Magic Pail

Ninnie-Dinnie seated herself on a bed of wild thyme close to where the hare had disappeared, and began calling very gently, but with great persistence :

' Skavarnak ! Skavarnak ! come into the Magic Pail ! Long-Eared ! Long-Eared ! come into my Pail !'

But nothing stirred in the bracken.

Long the child called—hours it seemed—until at last there was a movement under the great fronds of bracken, and out came a woebegone little hare and went into the Pail !

' You are caught by the magic of the Old Men's Pail at last,' said Ninnie-Dinnie, with a strange look in her eye ; and covering the Pail with her pinafore, she set her face homeward.

' Have 'ee got the hare ?' was Joan's greeting, as the child appeared in the doorway.

' I have,' she cried, with a ring of triumph in her voice.

' Aw, you poor little thing !' exclaimed Joan, eyeing the hare, who was gazing at her from over the Pail with a most dejected look in his dark eyes.

' Please don't pity *him*,' said Ninnie-Dinnie. ' He isn't really a hare: he is a dreadful little hobgoblin who has been cruel to all the dear Little People you love so much.'

' Who told 'ee all that, cheeld ?' asked Joan, looking at the little maid.

' P'r'aps the Wee Folk whispered it to me as I lay asleep in the costan,' answered the child.

The Magic Pail

When evening came, a most terrible wail came from the dresser, like the cry of a hurt child or an animal caught in a gin, which found its way at once to Joan's feeling heart.

'I can't a-bear to hear that cry,' she said to Ninnie-Dinnie. 'Do set the poor little creature free, that's a dear.'

'I can't, Mammie Trebisken, and I don't think I want you to, either. It is good for him to be kept prisoner in the Magic Pail.'

The hare wailed on, and poor Joan had to put her fingers in her ears to shut out the sound.

Tom came home just then, and, seeing there was a nice fat hare in the Pail, said he would soon stop his music, and that he would have him put into a hoggan for his dinner—a threat which so frightened the poor creature that there was no wail left in him for all that evening, and, leaning his head on the edge of the Pail, he looked exceedingly miserable, as I am sure he was.

The hare was kept prisoner in the Pail all that night and all the next day, and not even Joan gave him a look of pity, for even *her* heart was hardened against him.

When evening came again, he once more lifted up his voice in a loud and prolonged howl, which was almost more than the tender-hearted woman could bear, and she was about to ask Ninnie-Dinnie to give him his liberty, when a soft scamper of tiny feet made her turn her gaze to the open door, and in a

The Magic Pail

minute or less there appeared on the step three small hares, who, when they saw her pitiful glance on them, began to cry:

'Give us back our Daddy Skavarnak! Give us back our Daddy Long-Ears!'

'Hearken to *that*,' cried Joan, turning to Ninnie-Dinnie, who was preparing Tom's supper. 'I wonder you, of all people, can bear to hear it. Do 'ee give the little Skavarnaks their poor daddy.'

'You know I haven't the power,' said the little maid quietly, 'and I am afraid I shouldn't be very willing if I had.'

'But you wanted me to give the lark his music and his song and the pool its beams,' remonstrated Joan, as Ninnie-Dinnie shook her head. 'Why ever don't 'ee want the hare to be given back to his children?'

'I told you the Long-Eared had been very cruel to the dear Wee Folk. He was terribly cruel to one poor Little Skillywidden* in particular, and its mammie, to save it from further cruelty, had to hide it somewhere until he was caught in the Magic Pail. You see,' as Joan lifted up her pain-twisted hands in amazement, 'when he was taken prisoner by the Pail and brought into a good woman's cottage he became powerless to do the dear Little People any more harm, and all the spells that he threw over them became weak as money-spiders' threads.'

* A fairy's baby.

The Magic Pail

'What a wicked little creature he must have been!' cried Joan indignantly, shaking her head at the hare, who looked thoroughly ashamed of himself, and lolled his head over the edge of the Pail. 'But who told 'ee about the wicked Skavarnak an' his doings?' turning to the child, and giving her a searching look.

Ninnie-Dinnie did not answer, but a peculiar look came into her eyes and a smile played about her lips.

'I'm beginning to think our Ninnie-Dinnie is one of the Wee Folk her own self,' said Joan to herself, still gazing at the quaint little figure, with its dark, unfathomable eyes, and its elfin locks framing the gentle little face, ' an' that she is the Skillywidden its mammie hid for safety in a cottage. She is a dear little soul, whoever she is, an' I wouldn't part with her now—no, not for a bal full o' diamonds.'

As these thoughts travelled through her mind, the three little hares on the doorstep wailed out their entreaty again: 'Give us back our Daddy Skavarnak! Give us back our Daddy Long-Ears!' and the hare in the Magic Pail lifted his head and looked beseechingly at the child, who, however, took no notice of him.

The three little hares continued to cry on, and although it worried Joan's kind heart to hear it, she steeled herself against them on account of their daddy's cruelty, but into Ninnie-Dinnie's eyes there stole a wondrous pity.

The Magic Pail

'Poor little things!' she whispered to herself; and then, looking up at her foster-mother, she said softly: 'You may let the Long-Eared free if you like.'

'But I don't like,' said Joan severely. 'Why should I, when he have a-been so unkind to the dear Little People?'

'I would like you to give him his liberty if he will promise to go away from our moor and never come back any more for five hundred years,' continued the child, who apparently had not noticed the interruption. 'If he does not keep his promise after he is set free, he will run the terrible risk of again being taken prisoner in the Magic Pail and having Daddy Trebisken's threat carried out upon him.'

'What threat?' asked Joan. 'Aw, I remember now —his being put into a hoggan for my Tom's dinner. He is too *bad* for my good Tom to make a meal of,' shaking her head at the hare in the Pail. 'He will have to be made into a pasty, as a warning to all evil-intending Long-Ears.'

The poor animal in the Pail could not have looked more wretched if he was to be made into a pasty there and then, and he cried in his terror, and the three little hares on the doorstep lifted up their small voices in sympathy.

The latter's wails were more than Joan's tender heart could stand.

'Poor little things!' she cried, looking first at the small Long-Ears and then at Ninnie-Dinnie. 'If he will promise to do what you want him, I'll set him free. '*Tis* hard *they* should suffer for their wicked old daddy's wrongdoing.'

' It *is*,' responded the child in her gravest manner. ' And it is for their sakes more than his own that I am willing he should have his liberty. Ask him if he will consent to do all I told you.'

Joan, looking at the prisoner, repeated what Ninnie-Dinnie had said, and asked him whether he would have his freedom under those conditions.

The Long-Eared muttered something—what, she did not know, but the little maid seemed to understand, and she told her foster-mother that though the conditions were hard, he had promised to keep them if she would set him free from the Magic Pail.

' Then let us do it at once,' cried Joan, for the appealing eyes of those three little hares on the doorstep were more than she could endure.

The child came to her side, and offered her shoulder to enable the crippled woman to do her kind deed, and almost before Joan knew it she was at the door, with the Magic Pail gripped firmly in her hand, and found herself saying :

' I command thee, in the name of my little Ninnie-Dinnie an' the Magic Pail, never to come on our moors till the five hundred years are up. Remember, if you do, or try to hurt any of the dear Little People, they will compel thee to come into this here Pail, an' hand 'ee over to somebody who loves the Wee Folk as much as I do, an' who will

cut 'ee all to bits, an' put 'ee into a great lashing*
pasty for a miner's dinner.'†

The Skavarnak uttered a terrified howl, and Joan,
looking down into the Pail, saw, not a hare, but a
dreadful little hobgoblin, with ears as long as his
ugly little body.

She dropped the Pail in her fright, and the ugly
little creature sped away into the darkness, followed
by the three wee hares, or hobgoblins, as no doubt
they were.

Ninnie-Dinnie looked very happy when they had
gone, and the Pail evidently shared her joy, for it
was nearly white, and its embossed characters looked
almost as beautiful as the little Pool's sunbeams.

The child would not go out on the moor for a
long time after the Daddy Long-Ears was set free.
She said she must stop at home and look after her
Mammie Trebisken. But when October came, and
the purple heath-bells had changed to tawny brown,
and the bracken's green into orange and bronze, she
began once more to give little wistful glances out
over the great stretch of moorland.

One day—the very day of the same month she
was brought to the cottage in the bramble-basket
ten years before—Tom, noticing the longing glances,
begged her to go with him a little way, and Ninnie-

* Very large.

† Once upon a time the Cornish believed that his Dark Majesty
was afraid to come into the Cornish land for fear of being put
into a pasty.

The Magic Pail

Dinnie, after asking the crippled woman if she could spare her, got ready to go.

'I thought you wouldn't want to take the Pail along with you now the Long-Eared can't hurt 'ee any more,' said Joan, as the child went to the dresser for the Pail.

'And yet I *must* take it,' she replied. 'What shall I bring you home?'

'*Thyself*, my beauty!' cried the woman. 'I'm safe, I reckon, in wanting to have only my Ninnie-Dinnie brought back to me. She is better than all the lark's music an' the Pool's shine, isn't she?' appealing to Tom, who nodded his head. 'An' we don't want no Daddy Skavarnak here no more, do me?'

'I should think not,' cried the miner.

'Mammie Trebisken's request was a downright sensible one this time, wasn't it?' he remarked to the little maid as they walked away from the cottage.

Ninnie-Dinnie did not answer, which somehow troubled him, and he looked at her curiously.

When the miner and the child had reached the place where she had caught the hare, they stopped and looked about them.

The sun had risen, and was making everything beautiful on the moor—the little pools and all. It was a perfect morning for so late in the autumn. The dwarf furze, now in blossom, was burning like

The Magic Pail

gorse in springtime round the bases of the great grey carns; the bramble-vines were more beautiful than jewels, as they trailed in all their richness of colour over the boulders, and the gossamers lay thick on the turf and brown heather, and shone softly, as only gossamer can. Everything was very still, and there was not wind enough to stir even the blades of grass, nor was there anything on the wing save a seagull floating along on the blue air, and a few gorgeous Red Admirals hovering over their beloved nettles.

For ever so long Tom and the quaint little maid stood still, taking in all the wild, yet soft, beauty of the moors, until the latter broke the silence:

' I must hasten on to the bal now, my dear. You can stay here or go back to Mammie Trebisken, jest as thee hast a mind to.'

' Yes,' she said, with a start.

He glanced over his shoulder as he turned to go on his way, and, to his consternation, saw her put the Pail to her feet, and begin to speak in the same flute-like voice she had spoken to the Lark, the Pool, and the Hare, and the words were spoken to *herself*!

' Ninnie-Dinnie, give me thyself! Ninnie-Dinnie, give me thyself!' and the next minute he saw the little figure disappear into the Pail, which started at a rapid speed down towards his cottage.

He was too upset to go on to Ding Ding after that, and trembling like an aspen leaf, he followed in the track of the Pail; but whether he was Piskey-led, or what, he could not get home until dark, and when he got there, he found his wife sitting *alone*.

Three or four hours after Tom and Ninnie-Dinnie had left, Joan heard a little noise outside the cottage, so she told her husband when she related to him this strange story, and, looking up, saw, to her unspeakable amazement, the Pail a-walking down the road all by itself, as if it had legs, to the step of her door; and in another moment it had crossed the threshold and come to the fireplace where she was sitting gazing with all the eyes in her head at it coming! When it reached her feet it stopped, and looking into it she saw a very tiny Ninnie-Dinnie looking up at her with eyes full of love and pleading.

'Please, Mammie Trebisken, give me back *myself!*' she piped. 'Please, Mammie Trebisken, give me back myself!' and Joan took up the Pail in her crooked hands, and turning it over on its side, she cried:

'Ninnie-Dinnie, I give thee back thyself; an' come out of the Pail *to once!*' And Ninnie-Dinnie came out and stood before her, looking just as she had looked when she set out with Tom in the dawn. 'Whatever did 'ee let the Pail get hold of 'ee for?' asked Joan, when the child set the Pail in its place.

'Because you asked me to bring me back myself,' she said. 'And now I will sit at your feet and kiss your dear hands straight.'

The Magic Pail

Ninnie-Dinnie was very quiet the rest of the day, and when it drew towards evening and Tom's return, she asked if she might bring the costan to the hearth-place, as she felt so tired and sleepy.

Joan said she might, but was afraid it was too heavy for a dinky little maid like her to carry.

The child said she would manage to bring it some-how, and she did ; and when she had shaken up the moss and leaves in the costan she got into it, lay down, and was soon in a deep slumber.

Joan kept very quiet, so as not to disturb the poor little thing, and when she looked into the bramble-basket half an hour later, she saw something lying there that made her rub her eyes to see if she were dreaming.

In the place where Ninnie-Dinnie had lain down there was the most beautiful little creature it was possible to conceive. 'Its face,' as Joan afterwards told her husband, 'was ever so much sweeter to look at than a wild-rose, and its hair was softer and more silky than anything she had ever seen, even the head of the tom-tit ; and as for its mouth, it was far too tender and lovely even for her kissing. It had different clothes on, too, from what their little dear wore.' Joan said she could not tell what they were, only they were all goldy, like furze blossom.

Before she could get over her surprise at this little tiny thing in the bramble-basket, she heard a step outside, and thinking it was Tom come back from the mine, she looked up, and there in the doorway stood the same little bent old woman, her face hidden in a balbonnet, who had brought the child ten years before.

Before she could ask her what she wanted, the dinky woman had glided like moor-mist over to the hearthplace, and was bending over the basket and singing :

> ' Give me my Ninnie, my dear little mudgeskerry ;
>> The time is now up
>> For sweet-mead and cup,
>> For the Small People's dance
>> And the Nightrider's prance,
>>> The flute and the song,
>>> The horn and the dong,
> To welcome my dinnie, my little mudgeskerry !

> ' Give back my own dinky, my little pednpaley ;
>> The music's begun,
>> The frolic and fun,
>> The big stars are alight,
>> The full moon shines bright,
>>> The fairy lamps gleam,
>>> The Wee Folk all sing,
> " Come away to the feast, dear little pednpaley." '

' I *can't* give back my dear little Ninnie-Dinnie !' cried Joan, breaking in on the song, as it suddenly dawned upon her for what purpose the little old woman had come. ' Please *don't* ask me to do *that*. I have given back whatever else was asked of me gladly ; but I can't—aw, I *can't*—part with that dear little thing down there in the costan.'

The Magic Pail

The strange little body took no notice of the interruption, but went on singing ; and as she sang, the beautiful little creature in the bramble-basket opened its eyes and looked up at Joan with tender entreaty in them. That they were Ninnie-Dinnie's own little eyes looking up at her Joan did not for a moment doubt ; and she could but see they grew more wistful as the queer little woman sang on :

> 'Oh, seek not to hinder my own little Ninnie,
> For Magic and Pail,
> And the Long-Eared's wail,
> The free song of the Lark,
> And the light in the dark,
> The dinky herself—
> The wee little elf !—
> Have broken the spell o'er the dear little Ninnie !'

The Ninnie-Dinnie in the bramble-basket gave the crippled woman another look of entreaty as the voice of the singer died away. She understood that look so well, for she had appealed to her heart in that very same way when she had asked her to give back the Lark his music, the Pool its beams, and it made her feel now, as she felt then, that it was exceedingly selfish of her to want to keep what was not really her own, however desirable. And when the child, or whatever it was, met her gaze again she conquered her selfishness and resolved to give her back, whatever it cost her—'even,' she said, 'if it breaks my heart - strings.' And as the odd little woman in the mine-maiden's bonnet paused for a moment as if awaiting her will, in all the impetuosity of her generous nature she cried out :

' I give 'ee back your dinky, your little Mudge-skerry, your little Pednpaley, and whatever else you do call the little dear that you brought me ten years ago. I feel I've no mortal right to keep what don't belong to me, though I thought she did by this time. Take her if you *must*, an' thank 'ee kindly for the loan of her all these years.'

Joan's voice trembled as she uttered the last word, and the eyes of the lovely little Ninnie-Dinnie spoke their sympathy as she kept her gaze on her, and the funny little woman who had the voice of youth and the figure of old age showed hers in her voice, for she sang sweeter than before. It was an unfettered song, as unfettered as a lark's in the golden dawn :

'To the carns we will hasten, my little pednpaley.
Then let us away
That a birdie may
Fly down from th' Sky's Blue Nest
Above the shining West,
To the heart that's true,
To the heart that knew
'Twas better to give than to keep my pednpaley.'

As she was singing, Joan saw her glance over her shoulder at the Pail, which was all one shine on the dresser, and which, as she looked, left the dresser and came towards the fireplace and hopped into the costan!

As the last words of the song died away into the silence of the fire-lighted room, the little old woman in the bal-bonnet lifted the bramble-basket on to her back and glided out of the cottage as she had entered it; and the crippled woman, as she followed her with her eyes, saw hundreds and hundreds of dear Little People coming down the moor to meet her, singing and dancing as they came, and waving little white lights tipped with red stars, very much like the one that had shone from the Pail. When they came to where she stood they formed a ring around the quaint bent little figure with the costan on her back; and then she disappeared, and Joan saw in the centre of the ring, as the Wee Folk twirled in their dance, two tiny Little People more beautiful than all the rest—one of which she was sure was her Ninnie-Dinnie and the other the fairy who, in the form of a little old woman in a blue-grey cloak and a mine-maiden's bonnet, had brought her to her cottage that never-to-be-forgotten autumn evening.

Joan missed Ninnie-Dinnie dreadfully at first; but from the evening she gave her back, the rheumatism left her, and she was as well and strong as she was in the first years of her married life. And when autumn came round again, a dear little soft head of her own came to nestle close to her heart, and to make Tom and herself glad the rest of their days. But dear as this little Ninnie-Dinnie was, lovely as they thought her, they did not love her one bit more than that other Ninnie-Dinnie, the Skillywidden of the dear Little People, who were her friends for ever after.

Carn Kenidzhek.

The Witch in the Well

Padstow.

ONCE upon a time seven little maids of Padstow Town met together in Beck Lane to play a game called 'The Witch in the Well.' As they stood waiting for the child who was

The Witch in the Well

to act the witch, an old woman dressed in a steeple-hat and chintz petticoat came down the lane towards them.

'What are you doing here, my pretty maids?' she asked.

'Waiting for our witch,' answered the children, wondering who this strange-looking, oddly-dressed old woman could be. 'We are going to play "Witch in the Well."'

'Are you?' said the queer old body. 'I used to play that nice game when I was young like you, and should love to play it once again before I die. The little maid who was to have been your witch tumbled down on the cobble-stones in the market-place and hurt herself as she was coming hither,' she added, as they stared at her in amazement, 'and won't be able to play with you to-day. Will you let *me* be your witch instead of your little friend?'

'If you like, ma'am,' answered one of the children, after a hasty glance at her companions for consent.

'Thank you,' cried the old woman. 'It will be the most exciting game you ever played in all your life;' and, lifting her petticoats as if to display her high-heeled shoes and red stockings, she hobbled across the road to a well under a Gothic arch.

When the old crone had taken her seat inside the ancient well—and which was called the Witch's Well—Betty, the child who was to play the Mother in the game, took the other six little maids to a tumble-down cottage opposite the well, and the game began.

The Little Mother told her children—who were called after the six working days of the week—that she was going down to Padstow Town to sell her eggs, and that they must not leave the cottage, as the Witch o' the Well was about.

'Mind the old witch doesn't come and carry you away,' the wee maids said one to another when the Little Mother had gone.

As they were saying this, the old woman in the chintz petticoat and steeple-hat came to the door, and looked over the hatch.

'May I come in and light my pipe?' she asked.

'Iss, ma'am,' said Tuesday, unfastening the hatch; and when the old crone had come in and lighted her pipe, she crooked her lean old arm round Monday and took her away.

'Where is Monday?' asked the Little Mother when she had come back to her cottage, quick to see that one of her children was gone.

'An old woman came to light her pipe and took her away,' said Tuesday.

'It was the old Witch o' the Well,' cried the Little Mother. 'I'll go and see what she has done with her.'

And across the road to the well she went, and, stooping down and looking in, she saw an old woman sitting in the back of the well smoking a pipe.

'Where is my little maid Monday?' she demanded sternly.

The Witch in the Well

'I gave her a piece of thunder-and-lightning* and sent her to Chapel Stile to see if the waves were breaking on the Doombar,' answered the witch, knocking the ashes out of her pipe.

'I am off to Chapel Stile to look for Monday,' said the Little Mother, returning to the cottage. 'Be sure you don't let the old witch come in whilst I am away.'

Betty's back was no sooner turned than the same old woman came to the door.

'May I come in and light my pipe?' she asked.

'Iss, if you please, ma'am,' said Tuesday, forgetting her mother's injunction.

The old crone came in, lighted her pipe, and took away Tuesday!

'Mind the old Witch o' the Well don't come and take you away like she did Monday and Tuesday,' the children were saying to each other when Betty came back from her fruitless search for Monday.

'What! has the bad old witch come and taken away Tuesday?' cried the Little Mother. 'Dear! what ever *shall* I do now? I can't find Monday, and now my poor little Tuesday is gone!'

She rushed across the road to the well where the old witch was sitting, as before, calmly smoking her pipe.

'What have you done with Tuesday?' she demanded.

'I gave her a piece of saffron cake and sent her

* Bread and cream sprinkled with treacle.

The Witch in the Well

out to Lelizzick to ask Farmer Chapman to sell me a bag of sheep's wool for spinning,' the witch made answer.

'I am going out to Lelizzick to look for Tuesday,' said the Little Mother, rushing back to her children. 'Be sure you don't let the old witch come in. If you do, she will take you all away, and then what shall I do without my dear little maids?'

Betty was scarcely out of sight when a steeple-hat was seen at the window, and a pair of eerie eyes looked in.

Before the children could shut the door and its hatch, the old witch had come into the cottage.

'A puff of wind blew out my pipe,' she said. 'May I light it with a twig from your fire?'

'Iss,' answered Wednesday somewhat doubtfully. 'But Mother told us we were not to let you come in, because, if we did, you would take us away as you did Monday and Tuesday.'

'Did she?' cackled the witch, taking a bit of stick from the fire and thrusting it into her pipe. 'Well, I only want one of you now,' and looking round the room, her glance fell on Wednesday, and crooking her arm round her, she carried her off to the well.

'I have been out to Lelizzick and can't find Tuesday,' cried the Little Mother, coming into the cottage as the witch, with Wednesday under her arm, disappeared into the well. 'Oh! where is Wednesday?' looking round the room and seeing *another* of her children missing.

The Witch in the Well

' The old witch came in before we could shut the door, and took our little sister away,' said the children.

' This is wisht news, sure 'nough,' wailed the Little Mother, and off she rushed to the well, where the witch was sitting smoking.

' What have you been and done with Wednesday ?' she asked angrily.

' I gave her a bit of figgy-pudding, and sent her to Place House to ask if Squire Prideaux's housekeeper would kindly give an old body a bottle of their good physic to cure her rheumatics.'

' I'm going up to Place House to see if Wednesday is there,' said the Little Mother, looking in at the window of the cottage. ' If the witch should come to the door whilst I am away, don't let her come in, whatever you do !'

When she had gone to Place House, an old mansion standing above Padstow Town, the old witch left the well, and before the children saw her, she had pushed open the door, and stood in the doorway, looking in.

' May I come in and light my pipe ?' she asked.

' No,' answered Thursday.

But she came in, nevertheless, and having lighted her pipe, she caught up Thursday and took her across to the well.

' What ! has the witch been here again, and taken away Thursday ?' exclaimed the Little Mother when she came back from Place House without finding

The Witch in the Well

Wednesday, discovering that another of her children was gone.

'Iss,' sighed Friday. 'She came over the doorsill before we saw her.'

'This is too dreadful!' cried the poor Little Mother. 'I shall soon have no little maids left to call my own!' and wringing her hands, she went across the lane to the well.

'What have you been and done with Thursday, you bad old witch?' she demanded.

'I gave her a piece of limpet-pie, and sent her to London Churchtown to buy me a steeple-hat and a broom,' the witch made answer, rudely puffing her pipe in Betty's face. 'If you go there in Marrowbone Stage,* you will perhaps find her.'

'I am off to London Churchtown in Marrowbone Stage to look for Thursday,' cried the Little Mother, returning to her cottage in great haste and excitement. 'Keep the door and hatch locked and barred till I come back, and then, if you are good children and do as I bid, I will bring you home each a gold ring.'

When the Little Mother had driven away in Marrowbone Stage to London Churchtown in search of Thursday, Friday saw the witch leave the well and cross the road to their cottage.

'Shut the door quickly and bar it,' she cried to Little Saturday.

And Saturday had but slipped the bolt into its

* Legs.

socket when the old hag was at the door, knocking loudly to be let in.

' My pipe has gone out again,' she shrilled through the keyhole. ' May I come in and light it ?'

'*No !*' answered Friday. ' Mother said you would take us away as you did poor Monday, Tuesday, Wednesday, and Thursday, if we let you in.'

' I must come in and light my pipe,' insisted the witch. ' And if you don't open the door, I'll come through the keyhole ;' and as the children would not open the door, through the keyhole she came !

Having lighted her pipe and unbolted the door, she caught up both children and carried them away, and when the tired Little Mother returned from London Churchtown in a fruitless search for Thursday, she found to her dismay not only Friday gone, but dear Little Saturday !

She hurried to the well in an agony of despair.

' Where is Friday and Little Saturday ?' she cried.

' I gave them each a herby pasty,* and sent them to Windmill with grist to grind for to-morrow's baking,' answered the witch, spreading her petticoats over the dark water of the well.

' Tired as I am, I must go to Windmill to look for my dear children,' said the poor Little Mother, with a sigh. ' P'r'aps I shall meet them coming back ; and up the lane she went on her way out to Windmill.

* A pasty made of herbs.

The Witch in the Well

When she came back to the well the old witch had smoked her pipe, and was sound asleep and snoring.

'I have been all the way out to Windmill, and I could not see Friday and Little Saturday anywhere,' cried the Little Mother, shaking the old hag roughly by the shoulder. 'Where are they, you wicked old witch?'

'Friday and Little Saturday came back soon after you had gone to look for them,' said the witch, opening her eyes and yawning.

'Where are they?' demanded the Little Mother.

'With Monday, Tuesday, Wednesday, and Thursday,' answered the witch, knocking the ashes out of her pipe.

'And where is Monday and the others?'

'Upstairs,' answered the witch.

'Whose stairs?' asked Betty.

'*My* stairs,' returned the witch.

'Shall I go up your stairs and bring them?' asked the Little Mother eagerly.

'Your shoes are too dirty,' cried the witch.

'I will take off my shoes,' said Betty.

'Your stockings are too dirty,' protested the witch.

'I will take off my stockings.'

'Your feet are too dirty,' protested the old hag.

'I will wash my feet,' said the Little Mother.

'No water would wash them clean enough to climb up my stairs,' cried the witch.

The Witch in the Well

'I'll cut off my feet,' persisted Betty, determined that no excuse should stop her from getting to her children.

'The blood would drop and stain my stairs,' said the witch.

'I'll tie up my stumps,' cried the Little Mother.

'The blood would come through,' howled the witch.

'Then, what shall I do to get up your stairs?' said the Little Mother, with a cry of despair.

'*Fly up!*' cackled the old hag.

'But I can't fly without wings,' wailed Betty.

'Get wings,' cried the witch, with a sneer.

'How can I?' asked the poor Little Mother helplessly.

'I leave that to your clever wits to find out!' snapped the witch. 'And let me tell you that until you *can* fly you will never see Monday and your five other children again, nor get them out of my clutches!' And with a 'Ha! ha!' and a 'He! he!' the witch pulled her petticoats round her and disappeared under the dark waters of the well.

'My dear life!' ejaculated Betty, now really frightened. 'I believe that old woman who played the game with us was a *real* witch, and wasn't pretending at all, and has really and truly taken Monday, Tuesday, and all the others away.' And she sped away down to the quay where she lived with her terrible news.

There was a great to-do when the children's

'_" Fly up !" cackled the old hag._'

friends learned what had happened, and there was bitter woe and lamentation when, after days and days of searching, the poor little souls could not be found.

*   *   *   *   *

A year went by, and all this time Betty, the child who had acted the 'Mother' in the game, never forgot her six little friends. They were seldom out of her thoughts, and she longed for a pair of wings to fly up the witch's stairs; and the more she wanted wings, the more impossible they seemed to get.

One evening in the beginning of June—the very same day, as it happened, that she and her little companions had met together at the Witch's Well to play the game—she was passing the well, when a little white dog ran out of a garden close by, and came and licked her shoes.

She was fond of dogs, and, as she patted it, to her amazement it began to talk to her just like a human being, which almost scared her out of her wits.

'Please don't be afraid of me,' he said, wagging his stump of a tail as Betty backed into the hedge. 'I am only a dog in shape. I was a little boy before the dreadful old Witch o' the Well turned me into a dog, or what looks like a dog.'

'Were you really a boy once? And do you know the Witch o' the Well?' asked Betty, trying to get over her fears in her interest in what he told her.

'Alas, I do!' answered the dog. 'She is my mistress, and I have to follow her about all day long, and am never free of her except at night, when she is riding about on her broom. Then I have to haunt certain lanes to make silly superstitious people believe I am a ghost. The old Witch sent me to this lane a few days ago, and very glad I was, because I hoped to see you.'

'Whatever for?' asked Betty, still very much afraid of this strange dog, with his human-like voice.

'Because I know your little friends Monday and the others.'

'Do you really?' cried the child. 'I *am* glad!—Where are they?'

'In the witch's house, away on a dark moor, in her upstairs chamber,' answered the little white dog, with a wag of his tail, 'and where they will have to stay—so the witch says—until the little maid who played "Mother" in the game is able to fly upstairs after them.'

'Then, I'm afraid they will have to stay there always,' said Betty, her eyes filling with tears. 'Can't you get up the witch's stairs and bring them down?'

'The stairs are almost as steep as a tower,' answered the dog; 'and even if I could climb them, the door of the chamber where they are shut up is locked, and a spell worked upon the lock that nothing can open save a pair of wings and music.'

'What kind of music?' asked Betty.

'I haven't the smallest idea,' answered the dog. 'I only know that it has to do with you.'

The Witch in the Well

'Are my dear little friends happy?' asked Betty, hardly noticing the dog's last remark.

'They are most unhappy,' said the dog. 'They have nothing to cheer them, poor little souls, save the forlorn hope that perhaps one day their dear Little Mother Betty will be able to fly and get them out of the witch's power.'

'*The little white dog seemed to bend his head in thought.*'

'If I only knew how to fly, how quickly I would get up those stairs!' said Betty. 'There is nothing I can do, is there, to get a pair of wings?' she asked wistfully. 'Nobody who can help me to get wings?' she added, as the little white dog seemed to bend his head in thought.

The Witch in the Well

'Nobody but the Wise Woman of Bogee Down,' he answered, after considering a few minutes.

'I have heard of that strange old body,' said Betty. 'My mother often told me about her. She is very clever and wise, she said, and used to make simples for sick folks. She is terribly old now—a hundred and twenty, I think she told me.'

'That or more,' said the dog. 'But aged as she is, she is not too aged to work a kindness for anybody that asks her, particularly if it be against the Witch o' the Well.'

'Will she help me to get wings, do you think?' asked Betty eagerly.

'If it is within her power, I am certain she will,' returned the little white dog. 'Why don't you go and see her, and tell her the old Witch o' the Well has shut up six dear little maids, who were unfortunate enough to play the game with her a year ago, and that they cannot be set free until you, who acted the " Mother " in the game, can *fly* up to their rescue?'

''Tis a long way to Bogee Down,' answered Betty, 'but I'll go there to-morrow, all the same, if I can.'

'That is well,' cried the little white dog. 'You will not seek her help in vain, I am sure, especially if you tell her the witch's little white dog Pincher sent you. Now I must be off, for the old witch is up on her broom, and if she should happen to see us talking together, her horrid old cat would sclow*

* Scratch.

our eyes out. Good-bye, dear little Betty, and give
thee favour in the sight of the Wise Woman'; and
with another wag of his tail he vanished.

Betty hardly slept a wink that night, thinking of
her six little friends shut up in the witch's tower,
and so ardently did she desire wings to fly up to
their help that she got up and dressed before the
sun was risen. He was just rising over the golden
towans on the east side of the river as she left her
mother's house for Bogee Down, a wild, picturesque,
but lonely tableland about four miles from the ancient
town.

It was so early that nobody was up except herself,
and the doors of the Crown and Anchor were still
closed as she walked over the quay, down the slip,
and across the beach to the south quay.

The child went out of the town the nearest way
to the downs, up through a side road called the
Drang, and up Sander's Hill.

When she got up to Three Turnings, which
commanded a view of the river and Padstow low in
the hollow of the hills, she climbed a stile and looked
down to see if she could see the quay.

The river was now very beautiful with reflections
of the dawn, and its pale-blue water was flushed
with tenderest rose and gold. There was a flush
on the rounded hills, and a gleam of light on the
distant tors—Rough Tor and Brown Willy. There
was a ship in full sail coming up the harbour,

followed by a company of white-breasted gulls, which also caught the light.

The sun was high in the sky when Betty reached Bogee Down. Now she had got there she did not know in what part of it the Wise Woman lived. As she sent her glance over the wild down, gorgeous with yellow broom and other down flowers, she thought she saw blue smoke rising from a hedge a short distance up from Music Water, a delightful spot where Sweet-Gales, Butterfly Orchises, Bog-Asphodels grew, and where a clear brown musical stream ran down between the fragrant flowers, which made the place that June morning very beautiful.

The child went up over the down where she had seen the smoke rising, and found a hut huddled under a high blackberry hedge.

She knocked at the door, which was half open, and a thin cracked voice called out:

'Come in and tell me what has brought thee to this lonely down.'

Betty obeyed, but not without fear; and as she pushed the door open, she saw sitting in front of a peat fire on the hearthstone the bent form of an old woman with her back to the door. She was quaintly dressed, after the manner of ancient dames of the sixteenth century, and on her head she wore a cap as white as sloe blossom.

The old dame did not look round as Betty entered, but when the child had said all that Pincher the

little white dog had told her to say, and had asked
if she would kindly help her to get wings to fly up
the witch's stairs, she suddenly glanced at her over
her shoulder, with the brightest, keenest eyes the
girl had ever seen, and which seemed to look into
her pure young soul.

Evidently Betty's earnest little face pleased her,
for she smiled and said kindly :

'Pincher was a wise dog to send you to me. But,
let me tell you, you have asked me to do an almost
impossible thing. Yet, fortunately for those poor
shut-up little maids, it is not quite impossible; but
it will depend on yourself, whether your love and
pity for your little friends is strong enough to do all
that is required of you.'

'I'll do *anything* if I can only get wings to fly
with, and see Monday, Tuesday, and the others
again,' broke in Betty, with all a child's eagerness.

'Alas! the will that is strong and eager to do is
often weakened by the flesh that is frail,' said the
Wise Woman, with a shake of her head ; 'but the
question now is, Are you willing to live with me, an
old woman, in this out-of-the-way place, for a year
and a day, if 'tis required, and do all I bid you
willingly, without asking a single question ?'

'A year and a day is a long time to be away from
home,' said Betty honestly. 'Still, I am willing to
stay with you all that time and do your bidding if
my mother will let me.'

'That is well!' cried the Wise Woman. 'Now

go back to Padstow Town and get your mother's consent, and return to me to-morrow about this time.'

Betty's mother was very glad to let her little girl go and live with the Wise Woman, for she was very poor, and had twelve children.

The next day, when Betty was returning to Bogee Down, which she did by the same road as before, with her clothes done up in a bundle under her arm, who should she see, leaning over a gate, at a place called Uncle Kit's Corner, but the old Witch o' the Well, smoking her pipe!

'Whither away, my little dear?' cried the witch, as the child drew near the gate.

'To get a pair of wings to fly up your stairs to see Monday and the others,' answered Betty promptly.

'Ha! ha! That's too funny!' cried the witch. 'As well try to cut a piece from the blue of yon sky to make yourself a gown as to get wings to fly up my stairs.' And she laughed and laughed until she nearly choked herself.

'The witch may crow like an evil bird now,' cried the Wise Woman when Betty told her what the witch had said; 'but I shall hope to live to hear her screech like a whitnick* before that time has passed.'

When the little maid had undone her bundle, and put away her small belongings, the old woman told her to go to the settle, which stood by the fireplace,

* Weasel.

and take out from its seat a little bag of feathers, and separate one from the other and lay them on the table.

'That will be an easy thing to do,' said Betty to herself; and lifting the seat, she found a dinky bag stuffed full of feathers, rainbow-coloured, but so matted together that they were nothing but a soft ball.

'P'r'aps this is to make me a pair of wings,' said Betty; and seating herself on the settle, she set to work with a will.

But the feathers were not easily disentangled, as she soon found, and when evening came she had only succeeded in disentangling one tiny feather from the matted mass.

The Wise Woman neither looked nor spoke to her until the sun sank down behind the downs, when she told her to return the bag to its place in the settle, and then get her supper and her own and go to bed.

'I have only got *one* little feather to put on the table,' said poor little Betty, when she had put the bag back into its place.

'You have done better than I feared,' said the Wise Woman quietly. 'It is something to have untangled even *one* feather from its companions. It is a sign that it is quite possible that you may be able to fly.'

When they had had their supper, which consisted of black bread and goat's milk, Betty lay down in a bed made of dried grass and bracken, in the corner of the room, and slept the sleep of well-doing.

The Witch in the Well

' It will take me a whole year to untangle all these
feathers,' said the little maid to herself the next day,
when she again sat down to her task, which she did
when she had got her own and the Wise Woman's
breakfast, and had swept and sanded the hut.   ' 'Tis
dreary work, sure 'nough !'

' Pity, love, and patience will do wonders,' said
the Wise Woman, who seemed to have the gift of
thought-reading, and what she said comforted the
child not a little.

Every day for six long months Betty sat in the
settle most of the day separating feather from feather,
and it was not until the end of that time that the
last feather was laid upon the table, and so bright
and beautiful did they look that she said they looked
as if they had been dipped in a rainbow.

The Wise Woman did not tell her what they were
for, but she was sure they were to make her a pair of
wings.   ' And how beautiful they will be when they
are made—brighter than a sunset !' she whispered to
herself as she lay down to sleep that night.

When Betty awoke the following morning, she
looked at the table to see if the feathers were safe,
and saw, to her dismay, the Wise Woman sweep
them into the skirt of her gown and take them to
the door and shake them out on the down.

' Aw, my beautiful feathers !' ejaculated the child,
springing up in her bed, when as she did so the
ancient dame broke into a chant, and all she could
make out of it was that now the spell was broken

they must go with all speed to the Queen of the Little People and get her permission to help in the undoing of another spell.

When the chant had ceased, Betty, still more amazed, saw a great cloud, that looked more like winged flowers than feathers, float away over the downs towards the sea.

'I don't believe they were feathers at all!' cried Betty to herself. 'And, aw dear! how am I to get my wings *now* ?'

She longed to ask the Wise Woman to tell her why she had flung the feathers away, but remembering what the old body had said, that she was to ask no questions, whatever she saw or heard, she kept back the words on her lips.

She was very cast down when her work of many days was gone—she knew not whither.

When she had had her breakfast and had done all her little chores, the Wise Woman bade her search in the seat of the settle for a black stone, which, she told her, she must rub till it was the colour of life.

After much searching, she found the stone of curious shape wrapped in soft leather, which her old friend said she could use to rub the stone with.

Betty again set to work with a will, but rub as hard as she could, no rubbing seemed to affect the blackness of the stone, and at the end of a week it seemed *blacker* than ever. She was much troubled at this, and the Wise Woman, who read her thoughts, told her not to despair, as its blacker blackness was a sign that all would be well, and that she was in a fair way of getting wings to fly up the witch's stairs.

' How ?' was on Betty's lips, but a warning look from the Wise Woman's wonderful bright eyes made the question die unspoken.

For many a week longer the girl rubbed the sable stone—patiently and quietly most of the time, but there were days when she felt like throwing the stone out of the window and running away home to her mother. But pity for her poor little friends shut up in the witch's chamber made her persevere with her task.

One day, when she was almost worn out with rubbing, she saw a faint glow come into the stone, which, as she rubbed harder and quicker than ever, grew brighter and brighter, until it lay in her hand as red as a poppy.

' The stone is all afire !' she cried, taking it to the Wise Woman.

' It is the colour of life at last,' said the ancient dame, gazing at it with her wonderful bright eyes; 'and another spell loosened to the witch's undoing,' she muttered, half to herself. And noticing that Betty was listening with all her ears, she told the child to look in the settle for a box, and when she had found it to put it on the table and lay the stone within it.

There was only one box in the settle, which,

The Witch in the Well

though small, was most exquisitely carved all over with wings—wing interlacing wing—and as Betty set it on the table and put the stone into it, she thought she had never seen such a lovely box.

The next morning, when she awoke, she saw the Wise Woman at the door of the hut with the stone in her hand, and she heard her chanting : ' Go the way thy sisters went—the way of the west wind, and ask the King of the Wee Folk to give thee permission to help in the undoing of an evil wrought by the Witch o' the Well;' and Betty, staring with all her eyes, saw the ancient dame fling the stone out on to the down, along which it rolled at a rapid rate, burning as it went with a rosy splendour. It went the way the feathers had gone.

Betty dressed quickly, and busied herself about the hut, to keep herself from asking if the stone was really a stone, for she did not believe it was, and she ached to know.

When they had had breakfast, and the hut was cleaned with fresh scouring-sand, the Wise Woman asked her, if she had the chance of being made into a bird, what little bird would she like to be.

' A thrush,' said Betty. ' I should love to be a little thrush, because it sings so sweetly in the dawn.'

' It is a good choice,' cried the Wise Woman— ' the best you could have made. Now go down to Trevillador Wood, and every thrush you see in it, ask him to give you a feather for Love's sake.'

The Witch in the Well

'I do not know where Trevillador Wood is,' said the child, 'nor the way thither.'

'It is in a valley in Little Petherick,' returned the Wise Woman. 'It is not a great way from here, and easy to find if you follow a little brown stream from Crackrattle, that runs down through the valley to the wood. Crackrattle is away there, on Trevibban Down,' pointing to the opposite down, which was only separated from Bogee by a narrow road. 'By going up across Trevibban you will soon get to Crackrattle. Now go, my dear, and go quickly.' And Betty went.

The child was ever so thankful to be out of doors again, after having been cooped up in the hut for so many months, particularly as it was the birds' singing-time. Birds were singing everywhere on the downs, and their music gushed from furze-brake, from thorn-bush and alder; and when she came to Music Water she heard linnets fluting, and sweet wild notes came from budding willows by the side of the rippling stream. Larks were also singing— lark answering lark with such wonderful melody in the blue upper air that she told herself she had never heard such lovely sounds before.

The downs, in spite of all the bird-music, were not so beautiful nor so full of colour as when she came to stay with the Wise Woman. They were now as brown as Piskey-purses, she said, and only lightened here and there by granite boulders, where they caught the rays of the sun, by yellow gorse, and splashes of silver lichen.

It did not take the girl very long to cross Music Water's full stream to reach the road that parted the two downs; but it took her some time to get to Crackrattle, as the way up to it was thick with brambles and furze.

When she drew near that part of the down which commanded a grand view of the country and sea as far up as Tintagel, she turned her gaze towards Padstow Town, and saw the river twisting in and out of the hills on its way out to the open sea. She also saw the two great headlands, Stepper Point and Pentire, that guarded the entrance to Padstow harbour in that far-away sixteenth century, as they do to-day, and her glimpse of them and the blue river seemed to bring her home quite close to her; and when she reached Crackrattle stream, she followed it down the long, deep valley with a happy heart.

When she came to a wood, which she was sure in her mind was Trevillador Wood, she heard the thrushes singing and filling the place with music. Every cock thrush was doing his very best to out-sing his brother thrush. It was mating-time, and each little songster in speckled grey was trying to win a little mate by his song.

The first thrush that Betty saw—and he was a master singer and made the wood ring—was on the uppermost branch of a horse-chestnut just beginning to bud, and when he had finished his entrancing song, she lifted up her voice and said:

'Dear little grey thrush, please give me one of your feathers, for *Love's* sake.'

She wondered as she begged if the bird would understand her language; but he did quite well, and, what she thought was still more wonderful, she understood his!

'I will give you a feather gladly,' he piped in his own delicious thrush way. 'It is the beautiful spring-time, and the thrushes' courting-time; and because you beg a feather for *Love's* sake, I will pluck one that lies over my heart.' And the dear little bird did so, and flung it down into Betty's outstretched hands; and when she had caught it, he burst out into exquisite melody, and he was still singing, as she went down the wood lovely with budding trees.

From every thrush she saw she asked a feather for *Love's* sake, and she was not refused once, and by the time she had gone the length of the wood her apron was full of thrushes' feathers, plucked from breast and wing, tail and back!

'Were the song-thrushes willing to give their feathers?' asked the Wise Woman when Betty got back to the hut.

'Ever so willing!' cried the little maid, opening her apron to show what a lot she had got.

'It is more than enough,' she said. 'Put them into the box where the stone lay.'

The Witch in the Well

The following morning when the child awoke there was a mournful sound coming up from the sea, which they could command from the door of the hut, and the Wise Woman said it was a sign that a great storm was being brewed by the Master of the Winds, and that before the day was over he would send the great North-Easter across the land.

' I am sorry,' she said, ' as it will hinder our work, and perhaps I shall die the cold before we can help you to fly.'

Betty wanted terribly to ask the Wise Woman who beside herself would help her to get wings, but she dared not ask a single question, and felt it was very hard she could not.

Before the day had closed in, the bitter north wind, which was accompanied by snow, had come. It broke over the downs in great fury, and made the poor old woman shiver over her fire with the misery of it. The next day and the next it blew, and the more it blew, and the faster it snowed, the more the ancient dame shivered and shook; and all day long she kept Betty busy piling up dry furze on the hearth, till there was none left to put.

When she realized that all her winter store of peat and firewood was burnt, she moaned, and said she was sure she should die of the cold.

' And if I die,' she added sadly, ' the witch, like the north wind, will have it all her own way, and you will never be able to fly up her terrible stairs.'

This distressed the poor little maid very much;

for she had become quite fond of the Wise Woman, and wanted her to live for her own sake as well as for Monday's, Tuesday's, and the others'.

When the fuel was all burnt, and the Wise Woman too cold even to shiver, Betty said that when it stopped snowing she would go out on the downs and look for something to burn ; and when it stopped she went.

The downs were many feet deep under the snow, and there was not a furze-brake nor a hillock to be seen anywhere ; and the down opposite was as smooth as a sheet spread out on grass to dry.

As Betty was searching for wood, and could not find even a stick, a hare came speeding over the snow from Crackrattle. She watched it till it crossed over to Bogee, and saw, to her surprise, that it was making straight for her. When it drew near it stopped, with eyes that made her think of the witch's eyes, and as it gazed, the hare disappeared, and in its place stood the old witch herself, steeple-hat and all !

Betty was dreadfully frightened, and before she could rush back to the hut, the witch had come quite close to her, and asked her what she was doing out there in the cold.

' Looking for firewood for the poor old Wise Woman's fire,' answered Betty. ' And I can't see any,' she added sadly.

' Of course you can't,' laughed the witch. ' Sticks under three feet of snow are as difficult to find as a

furze-needle in a wainload of hay. It will comfort
you to know that you won't find even a stick, and
that before the north wind has turned his back on
the downs, the Wise Woman will have died of the
cold, and you will cry your eyes out for wings to
fly up my stairs!' And cackling and jeering, she
disappeared, and Betty saw a gray hare running
away over the snow down to Music Water, now as
silent as the downs themselves.

The little maid was returning to the hut with an
icicle of despair at her heart, when a white dog ran
across her path, and looking down, she saw it was
Pincher, the witch's dog.

'Don't let what my bad old mistress said distress
you,' he cried, licking Betty's cold little hand. 'She
does not want you to look for sticks, and came here
on purpose to prevent you. She is quite as anxious
that the Wise Woman should die as you and I are for
her to live. She is as clever as she is vile, and she
knows that a woman over a hundred could not
possibly live long in awful weather like this unless
she has a good fire to keep her warm.'

'But why does she want the Wise Woman to die?'
asked the little maid.

'Because she fears the wisdom of her long years can
help you to fly up her stairs. And this fear brought
her to Bogee Down to-day. She made me come with
her, which is fortunate; for poking about whilst she
was talking to you, I discovered a great faggot of
wood dry as a bone, and under it a pile of peat.'

The Witch in the Well

'Where?' Betty asked eagerly.

'Close to the hut under a hedge,' answered the dog. 'And if you will allow me I'll come and help you to get it out. The witch is so happy in her belief that she has discouraged you from looking for sticks that she won't miss me yet.'

And he led the way to the side of the hut, where, under a tangle of brambles, Betty saw a huge bundle of sticks, dry and brown.

They set to work with a will—she with her eager young hands, he with his strong white teeth—and soon got it out from under the hedge and into the hut, where, to their distress, they found the Wise Woman lying face down on the hearthstone, apparently lifeless.

Betty, girl-like, began to sob, believing the poor old woman was dead, which made Pincher quite angry, and he told her with a growl to put off her weeping till a more convenient time, and see if she could not kindle a fire with the sticks they had brought, whilst he tried to lick life back into her poor old body.

It was just the stimulus the child wanted. She mopped away her tears, and piled wood on the fire and set it alight; and Pincher, the dog, licked the poor old woman's face and hands with his warm, moist tongue.

Their efforts were not in vain, and they soon had the joy of seeing her open her eyes and stretch out her hands to the blaze.

'Thank you for all your kindness, dear Pincher,'

said Betty, when the dog said he must go. 'If I can ever do you a kindness in return, just ask me and I'll do it if I can.'

' Remember me when you can fly up the witch's stairs,' said the dog, with an appealing look in his eyes that Betty never forgot.

' Then you really believe I shall be able to fly up those stairs some day ?' she asked.

' I am almost certain you will, and so is the witch. You cannot live with people for generations without being able to read their faces. The witch's face is an open book to me now, and it tells me that she is not only afraid you will fly, but that it will happen soon. So fearful is she of this that a few days ago she actually wove another spell on the door leading up to the tower where the little maids who played the game are kept.'

' Do you ever get mouth-speech with the poor little dears ?' asked Betty wistfully.

' Never. But I sometimes see them at the barred window of their chamber. It isn't often they have time even for that, for the old witch keeps them spinning all day long. Farewell, dear! I *must* go. If the faggot of sticks is all burnt and the turf before the cold goes, don't go out again in search of more firewood. There is danger abroad. If the Wise Woman is in danger of sinking under the cold, just lay your warm heart against her heart, and all will be well.'

The dreadful weather still continued, and when

the faggot was all burnt, the dame again began to shiver and shake with cold, and said she should die this time, as there was no warmth left to keep life in her.

Betty was once more greatly distressed on her old friend's account, and declared she would go out on the downs to look for firewood in spite of what might happen to herself; but as she was going, the Wise Woman again tumbled, face down, on the fireless hearth.

As the girl picked her up (she was not the weight of a witch) and laid her on the settle, she remembered what the dog had advised her to do if the cold overcame the old woman again, and, lying down beside her, she pressed her warm young body against her aged body, and soon she had the joy of knowing that life was creeping back to the feeble old frame.

When the Wise Woman opened her eyes and saw the child's face close to hers, and felt her kind young arms about her, she said, with a tremble in her voice:

' Thou art a dear little maid. Thou hast rekindled the feeble flame of my life, proving to me that Good is greater than Evil, and Love stronger than Hate. I shall not die now before thou hast gotten thy wings. Get up, open the door, and call across the snow three times, " Little Prince Fire, come away from the Small People's Country and keep the Wise Woman warm till the cold goes !" '

Betty made haste to obey, and when she had opened the hut-door wide she called three times, as

' The stone was on the hearthstone, burning away like a faggot.'

The Witch in the Well

she was told, and then waited to see what would happen.

In a minute or less there appeared on the edge of the down a bright-red glow like a poppy in the eye of the sun. After burning there a minute or so it came like a flash over the snow towards the hut. As it came close, she saw it was the very same stone that she had rubbed for so many, many weeks.

It flashed like a ruby into the hut, and as it did so she thought she saw, through the soft rosy haze that seemed to envelope it, a tiny laughing face.

When she turned to see where the stone had gone, behold it was on the hearthstone, burning away like a tiny faggot, and the Wise Woman was sitting beside it with her withered old hands held out to the blaze!

It was so remarkable and queer that Betty could not at first believe the evidence of her own eyes, and rubbed them to make sure she was not dreaming. But it was no dream, for the miserable little hut, which a few minutes before was cold as Greenland, was now as warm as a zam* oven, and there was a soft glow all over it.

She sat down on the settle to enjoy the comfort of this wonderful fire, and she felt so warm and lovely after the terrible cold that it made her drowsy, and in a little while she was in a sound sleep. She never knew how long she slept, she only knew that when she awoke the wind and the snow had all gone, and the down birds were chanting a morning

* A hot oven that has been left to cool a little.

song outside the window. The stone was also gone, and the Wise Woman nowhere to be seen.

As she was wondering what had become of the latter, the old woman came into the hut with her apron full of green furze, and seeing the child wide awake, she cried :

'Get up, sleepy-head! The cold has left the downs this longful time, and the thrushes in Trevillador Wood have built their nests and are beginning to lay. Haste to the wood and get a bottleful of bird-music.'

'Where is the bottle?' asked Betty, getting up and looking about her.

'You will find one in the settle made of the Small People's crystal, into which you must ask every thrush you hear singing to his mate to drop a note to make a song with. Ask him to give it you for *Gratitude's* sake. When the bottle is full to its neck make your way back to the hut, and the first living thing you see after you have left the wood ask it to return with you to the Wise Woman. Ask it also to come for Gratitude's sake.'

After the child had eaten some food and had found the bottle, which was ever so tiny, and clear and bright as diamonds, she started for Trevillador Wood.

The cold had indeed all gone, as the Wise Woman had said, and the downs were all the better for the great storm that had swept over them. The snow had kept the earth warm, and had been a soft warm blanket to all the downflowers, and now the furze blossom was all manner of lovely shades of gold, and the soft spring air full of its fragrance. Music Water was all alight with marsh-marigolds, and the catkins of the grey-green willows were dusted with gold.

The snow had also been kind to the trees in Trevillador Wood (the Thrushes' Wood, Betty called it), and had wrapped all the baby buds and tender leaves in dainty white furs, and when the little maid entered the wood she saw, to her surprise, that most of the trees were dreams of beauty, with glistering leaves, and some of them were almost as brightly coloured as that strange stone, Little Prince Fire, as the Wise Woman had called it.

So delighted was she with all she saw that she forgot what she had been sent there for, until a thrush near startled the wood with a burst of melody. He was singing to his mate, for, drawing nearer, she saw, low down in a bush, a little hen thrush on her nest.

' Please, little grey-bird,* will you drop a note of your song into this bottle for *Gratitude's* sake ?' she asked, holding up the bottle to the singing thrush.

' Gladly,' piped he, ' especially as you ask it for Gratitude's sake. We have just received our first great blessing, which I may tell you is a tiny blue egg.'

' Give the child *two* notes,' piped a happy little voice from the nest. ' My heart is brimming over with joy for the warm wee thing under me.'

* The song-thrush is called the grey-bird in Cornwall.

The Witch in the Well

'Thank you for your kindness,' said Betty. 'But, if you please, little thrushes, the Wise Woman who lives on Bogee Down above Music Water, who sent me to this wood, said I must only ask for *one* note from each thrush I heard singing.'

'That is right,' chirped the little cock thrush. 'Always obey those older and wiser than yourself.'

'Ask the child what she wants thrushes' notes for,' chirped the voice from the nest. 'She didn't say, did she?'

'I forgot to tell you that,' struck in Betty. 'It is to make a song with.'

'I thought so,' piped the little cock thrush, and flying down, he put one of his most delicious notes into the tiny bottle, and in another second he was up on his bush again, singing deeper and more entrancingly than before, gratitude being the keynote and the chief utterance of his song.

Betty went down the wood with that music in her soul, and begged every thrush she heard singing to give her a note of his song.

Whether every bird's heart was also full of gladness for the freckled blue eggs in its dear little nest we cannot say, but they all gave willingly of their best, and before the child had gone through Trevillador Wood, the bottle of Small People's crystal was full to the neck with thrush-music.

Coming back, she saw two red squirrels sitting on their haunches at the foot of an oak-tree, eating nuts.

Said one squirrel to the other squirrel:

The Witch in the Well

'There is a dear little maid from Padstow Town here in the wood collecting music from the thrushes. It is the same child who, unknown to herself, undid a cruel spell which the Witch o' the Well cast over Prince Fire, a near relative of the King of the Little People. She turned him into a black stone, and a stone he had to be till somebody could rub it the colour of flame.'

'You don't mean to say so?' cried the other squirrel. 'This *is* news.'

'I thought it would be,' said the squirrel that spoke, arching his handsome tail with importance. 'Perhaps it will also be news to you to hear that this same little maid has actually untangled the dear Little Lady Soft Winds from that great Skein of Entanglement into which the wicked old witch tangled them, and from which nobody, not even the Wee Folk themselves, was able to free them.'

'However did she manage to do it?' asked the second squirrel.

'Only the Wise Woman of Bogee Down could answer *that* question. But the thrushes believe, and so do I, that love and pity for six little maids whom the witch has shut up somewhere gave patience to her fingers to do what the Wise Woman bade her do ; and because her heart was full of love for these poor little maids, whom she hoped by her obedience to get out of the witch's power, she unwittingly set free the other poor little prisoners—the Lady Soft Winds and Prince Fire, the King's cousin.'

The Witch in the Well

'And has she got her own little friends out of the power of the witch after all her love and patience?' asked the squirrel.

'Alas! not yet; but we all hope she will soon. The Small People are her friends now, especially those she set free. And it is told that they are going to turn her into a flying creature of some sort. Some say a bird, but nobody knows for certain. We are all on the alert to see what will happen. They say the Lady Soft Winds whispered to the daffodown-dillies last evening that Prince Fire had already begun to make a pair of wings for her to fly up the witch's stairs. But it may be only talk. And yet—there! the dear little maid is coming. Not another word, remember. She understands our language, and bird language too. The Wise Woman, it is said, put something on her tongue when she was asleep one day, when Little Prince Fire came from the Wee Folk's country to keep the Wise Woman's hut warm;' and then, catching sight of Betty's eyes bent upon him, he rushed up the trunk of the oak, followed by his companion.

'Well, those little funny things have told news, sure 'nough,' laughed the child to herself when the pretty little squirrels had vanished, 'and have told me all I ached to know without asking a single question. To think that the little feathers were the dear Little People; and that queer black stone was one too, and that they are going to help me fly up to Monday and the rest!'

The Witch in the Well

And she danced with delight as she thought of it, and the wonder was she did not dance the thrushes' notes out of the bottle.

When she was out of the wood, and walking up to Crackrattle, she remembered what the Wise Woman had told her, that the first thing she saw with wings she must ask it to return with her to the hut ; but the only winged creature that she noticed as she went up the valley was a large butterfly—or what she thought was a butterfly—on a great stone.

' The Wise Woman cannot want a butterfly to go back with me to her house,' said Betty to herself. ' But perhaps I had better ask it to come ;' and speaking gently, so as not to frighten away the lovely thing on the stone, she said : ' Little butterfly, please will you, for Gratitude's sake, come with me to the Wise Woman's hut ?' and to her amazement the tiny creature answered back :

' Gladly will I go with you. But, excuse me, I am not a butterfly. I am one of the Lady Soft Winds whom you freed from the tangle into which the old witch threw us.'

It began to rise on its azure wings as it spoke, and as it rose Betty saw it was indeed a fairy. It had the dearest little face she had ever seen, and as for its eyes, they were bluer than its own wings, and its soft, round cheeks were a more delicate pink than the cross-leaved heath that flowered on the downs early in the summer.

It flew on beside her, and Betty was so taken up

with watching it that she did not notice when she
got up to Crackrattle that a dozen other fairy-like
creatures were flying over the downs towards her,
until they were quite close.

'We are the Lady Soft Wind's sisters,' they said,
'and out of deep gratitude to *you* we have come to
go with you to the Wise Woman's hut.'

'Have you really, you little dears?' was all Betty
could find words to say. 'Come along, then.'

And they came, and were a rhythm of colour as
they flew beside her, or, as the child expressed it,
'a little flying garland of flowers.'

Thus accompanied, Betty came to the hut, where,
in the doorway, stood the Wise Woman, leaning on
her stick, evidently awaiting her and her companions'
arrival.

'We have come,' said one of the little creatures.

'I felt certain you would,' said the Wise Woman,
making a curtsey, 'and a thousand welcomes. If
the child has brought the thrushes' notes everything
is ready.'

'She has brought them,' put in another tiny voice,
'and they are impatient to sing.'

'Then please follow me,' said the Wise Woman,
going into the hut ; and in flew all the lovely little
creatures, with gentle fanning of wings, which made
a soft breeze as they came.

'Prince Fire is already at work,' said the Wise
Woman, pointing to the box, and Betty, who had
followed the Little Lady Soft Wings, saw, sitting in

the box amongst the thrushes' feathers, a small person dressed in red, busy making wings! He was Little Prince Fire, and a very great person in the Small People's World.

'My dear life! aw, my dear life! What shall I see next?' cried the little Padstow maid to herself; and what more she would have said is not known, for at that moment the Wise Woman took the tiny crystal bottle out of her hand and put it into the box beside the dinky person within.

'The Lady Soft Winds have arrived, your Royal Highness,' she said, 'and Betty, the little Padstow maid, is also here.'

'Good!' piped the tiny man. 'Bid them sing the Making Song.'

'We require no bidding, Prince Fire,' said a little Lady Soft Wind, with gentle dignity, as she and the others alighted on the table. 'Out of gratitude and love we have come from afar to sing this song, knowing well, unless we sang it, you would never complete the wings. We, as well as you, can never repay the little maid of Padstow Town for releasing us from the witch's spell.

The voice had hardly died away when all the radiant fairies began to wave their wings, at first slowly, and then rapidly, in a kind of rhythm, and sang very softly as they waved them.

Betty watched them with all her eyes, and whether it was the movement of their wings or the curious song they sang, with its hush-a-by kind of tune, she

felt ever so drowsy, just as she had felt when Little
Prince Fire blazed away like a faggot on the hearthstone, and sitting down on the settle, she fell asleep
with the two first verses of the song in her ears:

> 'We Wee Folk together
> With music and feather
> The gift of the birds—
> The little grey-birds—
> Do make her a thrush
> All sweetness and gush.
> > Lallaby ! Gallady !

> 'And the Little Prince Fire
> Her sweet song will inspire,
> That she may fly high
> Where little maids sigh,
> And undo the spell
> Of the Witch o' the Well.
> > Lallaby ! Gallady !' '

The next thing she heard was the Wise Woman
telling her to rise up and move her wings, and
Betty, nothing loth, lifted herself from the settle
and found she was all air and lightness, like the
Little Lady Soft Winds themselves, and could fly
about the hut with the greatest ease; the feeling of
flying was altogether delightful!

The Lady Soft Winds watched her flight with
the deepest interest, and Prince Fire, who was
sitting on the edge of the carved box, watched too;
that he approved of her flying powers it was plain
to see, for his bright eyes never left her wings.

'What am I now?' asked Betty at last, perching

The Witch in the Well

on a beam, and looking down sideways bird fashion on the Wise Woman.

'You are a little grey thrush,' said the Wise Woman, her withered face a big smile.

'And now, little grey thrush, away to the east, where the witch's house looms out dark and strong against the gold of the morning sky,' said the Lady Soft Winds, 'and fly up her terrible stairs and set your six little children free, as you did us.'

'Yes; away to Monday, Tuesday, and Wednesday,' cried Little Prince Fire.

'And Thursday, Friday, and Little Saturday,' struck in the Wise Woman.

'Away, away, little grey thrush!' cried they all, singing as they cried. 'The sun is rising behind the Tors, and the time is come for *our* little thrush to fly and sing. Then, away, away!'

Their little thrush wanted no further urging, and with one full, clear, melodious note, which filled all the small fairies with delight, it flew out of the hut, followed by the gentle winnowing of the Lady Soft Winds' wings.

So glad was Betty, the little grey thrush, at being on her way to see those dear little maids that she flew faster than ever thrush flew before, and the sun was not yet over the Tors when she reached a grim old house standing all alone on a brown and desolate moor, with its back to the golden sunrise.

Instinct told the little grey thrush that it was the witch's house, and alighting on a blasted tree, close to its spell-bound door, she began to sing with all her might; and so joyous and so triumphant was her song that it seemed to bring gladness and hope even to that desolate spot.

As Betty, in her bird form, sang on, the old witch came round the corner of her house, dragging her unwilling feet as she came. When she lifted her bad old eyes and saw a grey thrush high on the tree, singing with all its cheerful heart, she turned green, and hearing the door of the tower leading up the stairs—where Monday and all the other little maids were shut up—groaning as if in pain, she sank in a heap on the ground, and began to groan and moan too.

The bird sang on, and its whole body was one shake with its music, and the more thrilling was its song, the more the witch moaned and groaned. Then, when its last triumphant note rang out, the great door opened, as if pushed back by some magic power, and revealed a flight of very steep stairs. The witch gave a piercing howl when she saw the door open wide, for she knew that the small grey thrush's music had broken her spells, and that she was completely in the power of that little singing bird.

When the door of the tower was as wide open as it could go, the thrush gave three flaps of its wings, and then it flew out of the tree, and in through the doorway of the tower, up and up the witch's stairs. And at the top of the stairs was a small room, where six little maids sat spinning.

The Witch in the Well

They were so busy, and the hum of the wheels was so loud, that none of them noticed the entrance of the grey-bird until it broke into a song from the window-sill.

'Why, it is a dear little thrush!' cried Friday, who was the first to notice it. 'How ever *did* it get up here? 'It must be the bird we heard singing so beautifully outside just now;' and all the children stopped their spinning-wheels to look at it.

'Did it really fly up the witch's stairs?' asked Thursday, resting her sad, soft eyes on the thrush, whose heart was beating so against its speckled breast at the sight of those dear little maids that it couldn't tell them at first who it was.

'It did,' answered Monday, 'and its flying up here makes me think of our Little Mother Betty, who played the game with us. Will she ever be able to fly up the witch's stairs, I wonder?'

'I am afraid not,' said one of the other children, with a sigh. 'I have given up all hope of her ever doing that now.'

'You are wrong, my dears,' cried the thrush, finding its voice at last. 'I am Mother Betty, turned into a dinky bird for your sakes, and have flown up the witch's stairs!'

And it flapped its wings, jerked its tail, and behaved altogether in a most extraordinary manner, for the children's faces of amazement and hope nearly sent it mad with joy. And then, as if it must relieve its feelings still more, it burst into a most enchanting song, which was answered outside the tower by a series of joyful barks from Pincher, the witch's dog.

'It *must* be Little Mother Betty,' said Monday, leaving her spinning-wheel. 'I can hear her own voice in the song.'

Then all the other little maids left their wheels to gaze at the bird.

'Are you *really* Betty who played the " Witch in the Well " with us that terrible day ?' they asked.

'Indeed I am,' sang the thrush. 'I have come to take you away from here. Now follow me down the stairs and out of the house.'

'The stairs are so steep,' began Saturday, with frightened eyes.

'Don't be afraid, dear little Saturday,' sang the bird. 'It will be as easy as thinking. Come along, all of you.'

The six little maids followed the bird out of the room and down those wall-like stairs, and in a minute or less were outside the witch's house, where they found the old hag in the act of mounting her broom.

They were met at the door by Pincher the dog, who welcomed them with joyful barks and wagging of tail ; and then, finding his mistress had fled, he looked up at the little grey thrush, who was wheeling round and round the children's heads out of sheer gladness, and begged her to give chase to the witch. ' For,' said he, ' if she goes out of your sight before you have commanded her to do something, you are in danger of having to retain your thrush-shape.'

'I am glad you told me,' said the thrush, and it was about to fly after the witch, when it recalled to

'*Over the moor and across the downs they all went.*'

mind what the dog had said the day he helped to drag the faggot of wood into the hut: 'Remember me when you have flown up the witch's stairs.' 'I have been up the witch's stairs and down again,' it said, alighting on the ground beside him. 'Is there anything I can do for you, Pincher ? I am here to do it if I can.'

'I long to be set free from the power of the witch,' said the little dog, fixing his gentle eyes on the bird, 'and to be restored to my own shape. If you bid the witch do this, though it will be vinegar and gall to her, she is bound to obey you by the merit of your wings and your song. I long exceedingly to be myself again.'

'You shall,' sang the little grey thrush.

And then, telling the children to mount Footman's Horse* and follow hard after her and the witch, it flapped its wings again, and flew after the old hag on her broom, and Pincher the dog and the six little maids sped after them.

Over the moor and across the downs they all went like the wind, the witch keeping well in advance. Uphill and downhill and through the lanes they flew, and never once did they stop till they came to Place Hill, where the great stone gateway of Place House stood greyly out from a background of beech-trees and oaks. Here the six little maids stopped to get breath, but the old hag, though ready to drop from her broom with fatigue, paused not a second, and went on down the hill with little Thrush Betty, and Pincher the dog close behind her.

'The witch is out of sight !' cried Monday, as the old hag and the little grey-bird disappeared round a corner.

* Their legs.

The Witch in the Well

' So she is !' said Friday.

And they all whipped up their tired little steeds, and away they sped down the steep hill in pursuit of the witch; but they did not overtake her until she got to the well, when they stood watching to see what would happen.

The old hag slid off her broom, and, looking cunningly about her, as if in search of the thrush, which was on top of the wall above the well, she made a quick step to the well, and put her foot on its ledge.

' Sing, sing, dear Thrush Betty !' cried the small white dog in great distress, or the witch will disappear into the well before you can command her to do what you said.'

And Betty, the little grey-bird, flew into a tree, and began to sing with all its might once more. And as it sang, the old hag crept back from the well, and stood in the middle of the road, with a terrible look on her face.

Now, being a witch, and one of the worst of her kind, she could not endure anything so pure and sweet as the small bird's song; every note it sang ·was an agony to listen to, and, knowing in her wicked soul that its music had crushed all her evil power, she begged permission in a humble voice to be allowed to go into the well.

' You may go,' sang little Thrush Betty; 'with one condition, which is that you turn Pincher back into a boy !'

The Witch in the Well

'Please ask me something less hard!' pleaded the witch, cringing before the little bird. 'Pincher will be mine no longer if I do that, and I cannot do without my faithful little dog. Where I go, he must also go.'

'That he shall not!' sang the thrush. 'I command you, by the merit of my wings and the power of my song, to remove your spell from this poor little boy!'

'To lose my little white dog is worse than having the Lady Soft Winds and Prince Fire set free from my spells!' muttered the witch. 'Worse even than losing the six little maids who played the game with me and did all my spinning.'

'Give him back his own self this very minute,' sang the little grey thrush, 'or else——'

If a threat was implied in the sentence, the witch understood it, for, with a howl of rage, she made a pass with her broom over the dog. As she did so, the dog vanished, and in its place stood a young boy, dark and very handsome, dressed in clothes of a bygone age!

The six little maids stared at him in open-mouthed astonishment, and as they stared as only little maids can, the witch made for the well.

'Please sing once more, little Thrush Betty,' cried the boy in a voice it knew so well. 'This last song will quite end the power of the bad old witch, and keep her down in the bottom of the Witch's Well until she repents of all she has done.'

'That will be never!' snarled the witch; and with

a horrible cry, which even the victorious song of the little grey thrush could not drown, she splashed into the well. And when Monday, Tuesday, and the other little maids could get that cry out of their ears, the well and its quaint old arch were no longer to be seen, and near where it had stood was dear little Betty, their friend, who had played the 'Mother' in the game, looking very little altered, only a few inches taller, and standing beside her, holding her hand, was the boy, who, in his dog-shape, had done so much for them all.

'Now let us go home to our mothers,' cried Friday.

'I have no mother to go to,' said the boy sadly, as he hesitated to go with the happy children. 'Mine died long ago, and I have no home.'

'Our mothers shall be your mother,' cried the little maids, 'and you will never lack anything if you come with us.'

So they all came down through Padstow Town, the boy in their midst.

Nobody noticed them till they reached Middle Street, a straight cobbled street with quaint houses on either side, when a 'Granfer man'* spied them, and shouted the news that the long-lost children had come back, and the whole street rushed out to welcome them.

Thursday lived at the bottom of this street, and Betty thought she ought to see her safely home; but the child's mother had already heard of their

* A *very* old man.

arrival, and came out to meet them and to clasp her own little maid to her heart.

Monday's home was in a narrow street called Lanedwell, and when she was safe within her parents' house and arms, the other five little maids and the handsome boy, accompanied by a great crowd, went on their way to the market, where Saturday lived.

As they came out of Lanedwell Street, a house across the market stood full in view. It was one of the quaintest of buildings, of Tudor date, with an outside flight of stone stairs leading up to its side entrance under the eaves. Little Saturday's eyes glistened when she caught sight of this house, for it was her own dear home. Her father happened to be at the top of the stairs looking over the wooden rail as the children drew near, and he nearly fell over into the street below when he saw his own long-lost little maid.

Through a narrow passage, called the Blind Entry, the children and crowd of people poured, and they only got through when Saturday's father was down the steps and over to the Entry to greet them.

'There is the "George and the Dragon"!' cried Thursday, pointing to an inn at the bottom of a street as they crossed the market.

'Iss,' said Betty, with a smile; 'and St. George is *still* slaying the Dragon!' gazing up at the sign hanging above the door.

The Witch in the Well

'Perhaps the Dragon is even more difficult to conquer than the Witch o' the Well,' put in the boy, eyeing with great interest the inn's sign, on which was painted in glowing colours England's patron saint, with uplifted sword to slay the Dragon.

'Ever so much more, I reckon,' responded Betty.

Another small street brought them to the quay, where the other four little maids' homes were, as well as Betty's, and to their exceeding joy they saw their fathers and mothers and all their relations and friends coming to meet them. And what a meeting it was, and what a welcome they had!

Never since the day when the two ships, which the people of this ancient town sent fully equipped to help in the siege of Calais in Edward III.'s reign, came safely back was there such rejoicing, so the old 'granfer men' said.

Every vessel in the harbour hoisted its flag in honour of the children's return and the overcoming of that wicked old witch.

The boy, when Betty told how she had got her wings that enabled her to fly up the witch's stairs, was made much of by the people of Padstow Town, and the friends of those seven little maids almost fought who should have him for their own.

How it was settled there is no need to tell, save only that he lived on Padstow quay, and that he and Betty were always friends and loved each other dearly; and when they grew up they married, and were as happy as the summer is long.

Borrowed Eyes and Ears

Tamarisk Lane.

IN a lane where red-stemmed tamarisks grew lived another Wise Woman. She was a nice old body, as many of her kind were, and, like them, was well acquainted with the healing properties of herbs and blossoms—revealed to them, it was said, by the fairies. But this Wise Woman was not at all liked; nobody seemed to know why, except that she could do many wonderful things her neighbours could not, and was, moreover, very ugly. People were even afraid of her, and never went near her cottage unless they wanted to buy her herb physic, ointments, and that sort of thing. But there was one who was not afraid of her at all, and that was a dear little girl called Bessie Jane Rosewarne, the only child of a farmer who lived near Tamarisk Lane.

This little maid had a kind heart, especially for those who were lonely or sad; and when she knew how lonely the poor old Wise Woman was, she often went to see her, and took her little presents in the shape of fruit and flowers.

Annis, as the old woman was called, soon got to be very fond of the kind-hearted child; and to show how she appreciated her kindness she used to tell her stories about the Small People and the dear little brown, winking Piskeys, whom she seemed to know very intimately.

Bessie Jane was always interested in the Wee Folk, particularly the cliff ones and the sea-fairies, and expressed a great desire to see them.

Early one afternoon the child brought her old friend a basket of red currants and a cup of cream; and when she had set her gifts on the table, the Wise Woman went to her dresser and took from it a very

small shrimping-net, or what looked like a shrimping-net.

'It is a present I have made for you, dear little
maid,' she said.

'What is it for?' asked the child, when she had
thanked Old Annis for her gift. 'It looks like a
shrimping-net, only its meshes are so fine—as fine as
gossamer—that I am afraid it will not bear even the
weight of a baby-shrimp!'

'It is stronger than it looks,' said the Wise
Woman, with a curious look in her sloe-black eyes.
'Its meshes are made out of Piskey-wool, which the
Small People spun on their own little spinning-
wheels, and which they gave me to mesh into a net.
Its hoop and handle I cut from an ash-tree, where
the Wee Folk gather to hold their gammets* in the
moonshine.'

'Did you really?' cried little Bessie Jane. 'How
very interesting! I shall go down to Harlyn Bay
at once and catch shrimps in the great pool under
the shadow of the cliffs there.'

'It will catch something nicer than shrimps, I
hope,' said Old Annis, following the child to the
door. 'Whatever you catch in it, my dear, don't
let it get out of the net until it promises to lend you
its eyes and its ears for a night and a day.'

'I don't think I want anyone's eyes and ears but
my own,' laughed the little maid as she went down
Tamarisk Lane, which led to Harlyn Bay, swinging

* Games.

170

the shrimping-net as if it were a common net, and not spun from Piskey-wool by the Small People and made by a Wise Woman.

The bay, with its great beach of golden sand, its many hillocks—silvery-blue in places with sea-holly, and green with clumps of feathery tamarisk—lay open before her as she came out of the lane. There were many gulls on the wing to-day, white as the waves that broke gently over the rocks and against the sides of the cliffs. She looked about her, as was her wont, when she reached the beach, but there was nobody on the bar save an old man with his donkey, its panniers full of sand, coming up the beach on the way back to Higher Harlyn, where he lived.

Bessie Jane made straight for the pool of which she had spoken. It was a very deep pool, full of sea-anemones, shrimps, and lovely seaweed, and in the centre of the pool was a rock, in the shape of an arch, covered with mussels.

As the child was about to dip her net into the pool, she saw a streak of silver dancing up and down in the clear water.

She watched it for a minute, and then she thought she would try and catch it, and leaning over the pool, she put her shrimping-net under the whirling brightness and caught it. Looking into the net to see if it were a fish, to her great delight she saw it was like one of the tiny sea-fairies Old Annis had told her about. It was a most beautiful little creature; its eyes were the colour of the Cornish sea at its bluest, and its hair, which was a pale shade of gold, was sprinkled all over with sunbeams. It had no clothes on save a little green shift!

'Oh, you dear little darling!' cried Bessie Jane, after gazing at the lovely atom sitting in her shrimping-net. 'I came down here to this bay to catch shrimps, and I do believe I've caught a sea-fairy instead!'

'You have,' piped the little creature in the most silvery of voices; 'and woe is me that I am the first of the sea-fairies to be caught in a net!'

'I hope you don't mind very much,' said Bessie Jane, looking uncomfortable. 'I have never seen a fairy before of any sort, and I have been longing to see a little sea-fairy like you. The Wise Woman who lives in Tamarisk Lane, near our farm, told me about the sea-fairies. It was she who made me the net, which she meshed her own self out of Piskey-wool spun by the dear Little People.'

'That explains my being caught in a net!' cried the little creature, with a sigh of relief. 'I do not mind so much now—that is, if you will put me back into the pool. You will do me that kindness, won't you? I and my little companions were playing Buck and Hide Away here in the bay when the tide was in, and as I was hiding under the rock in the pool where you netted me, the tide went out and left me behind. You see that great bar of sand'—pointing at it with her tiny pink finger, which was even a more delicate pink than the beautiful tamarisk

' She put her shrimping-net under the whirling brightness and caught it.'

blossom that makes Tamarisk Lane and all the other lanes near Harlyn Bay so pretty in the summer and autumn months—' it is a terrible thing to us little sea-fairies,' as Bessie Jane nodded. ' We have not the power to get over sand-bars. My companions are in a wisht* way about me, knowing all the dangers that beset us when we are cut off from the sea.'

' You must not be afraid of me,' Bessie Jane hastened to assure her, thinking the little sea-fairy's words were meant for her. ' I wouldn't hurt a hair of your bright little head. And if I can't do what you ask me, it is because I love you so much, and want to take you home to our farm. We live in such a dear old house ! I would be ever so kind to you, and you should be my own dear little sister. It would be lovely to have you to play with !'

' I am sure you are very kind,' said the sea-fairy in a voice that trembled. ' But, dear little maid, I couldn't be happy anywhere away from my relations and friends, and I couldn't live out of the sea very long, and if you were to take me to your house and keep me there I should fade away and vanish with fretting.'

' Would you really ?' cried Bessie Jane. ' Then I won't take you to my home. If you like, I'll carry you down the sand and put you back into the sea.'

' Oh, will you, dear little girl ?' cried the tiny creature joyfully, her eyes growing as bright as her

* Sad.

hair. 'I will be always grateful to you if you will. My little brothers and sisters and crowds of my friends are in the sea close to the shore watching me.'

'I can't see them,' said Bessie Jane, turning her gaze seaward. 'I can only see sun-sparks on the edges of the waves.'

'They are sea-fairies,' said the wee creature. 'You can't see their forms, of course, and you would not have seen *me* if I had not been caught in a net made out of Piskey-wool spun by the Small People and meshed by a Wise Woman. Will you please take me down to the sea now? It seems ages since the tide cut me off from my dear ones.'

'I will this very minute, if you will lend me your eyes and your ears for a night and a day,' answered Bessie Jane, remembering Old Annis's injunction.

'I will do what you ask gladly,' said the little sea-fairy, 'for I am very grateful for your kindness in offering to take me back to my friends. When you have put me into the sea a wave will bring to your feet a little red ball, which will contain my ears and my eyes, and which you must take to the Wise Woman, who will keep them until sunrise to-morrow.'

Bessie Jane carried the little sea-fairy very carefully down the sandy beach in the shrimping-net, and when she had put her into the sea, the water all around her broke into white fire, and a soft, sweet sound, like the coos of young pigeons, filled the air;

and then, as the brightness enclosed the tiny creature, she disappeared—ears, eyes, and all !

'Oh, the sea-fairy has forgotten her promise,' cried Bessie Jane, gazing dolefully at the spot where she had sunk.

As she was speaking, a wavelet broke at her feet, and looking down, she saw a round ball of airy lightness and brightness lying on the sand. It was red as pools when the sun sets, and the child picked it up and looked at it, and through its almost transparent skin she saw a shadow of ears and a glimmer of something blue; and she took it to the Wise Woman, as the fairy had bidden her.

Old Annis smiled when the little girl told her what she had caught in the shrimping-net.

'It was what I had expected,' she said. 'Now, dear little maid, you must get up with the larks to-morrow and come here, and you shall then see what you will see.'

Bessie Jane got out of bed the minute she awoke the next day, which was just as the little skybirds were beginning to sing ; and when she was dressed she hurried off to Tamarisk Lane.

Early though it was, the Wise Woman was also up, and when she saw her little friend coming, she went and opened her door.

The first thing the child saw as she came into the cottage were two tiny ears—smaller even than a harvest-mouse's ears—on the table, and near them two round eyeballs, with a sapphire spark in each of them.

As her glance rested on the wee eyes and ears, Old Annis called her to her side, and taking up the ears, she dropped them into the child's ears; then she took up the eyes, and putting some Wee Folk's glue on their back, she put them into Bessie Jane's pretty brown ones, and told her to look round her cottage.

The child did so, and saw to her amazement that it was full of Small People, including little Brown Piskey-men. They were all amusing themselves in various ways: some were running about the sanded floor; some were looking into the depths of a Toby jug full of milk; and some tickling Old Annis's large grey cat. The Piskeys were astride her fiddle-backed chairs and her settle, and winked at the sweet little maid whenever she turned her gaze their way, and they winked so funnily she could not have helped laughing to save her life. As she was looking at them, the Wise Woman told her if she wished to see the sea-fairies in Harlyn Bay she must go at once.

She did not at all want to go, for the Small People were most fascinating, she told the old woman, particularly the little brown winking Piskeys; but she went all the same.

As she walked down the lane to the bay, she looked through the tamarisk hedge into the common, and saw that somehow or other it looked different. There was a soft green light hanging over it, and where the sand was only the day before there was a multitude of most beautiful flowers of every colour and shade, the like of which she had never seen before. Amongst the flowers cows were feeding. The cows were ever so small, not bigger than rats. There were teeny tiny goats there, too, and dear little men in queer hats and coats looking after them. The cows and goats belonged to the Wee Folk, she supposed. It was all so delightfully different and odd, and she couldn't think how she had never noticed all this on the common before, till she remembered she was seeing through a sea-fairy's eyes.

As she climbed the cliffs overlooking the bay a sound of sweetest music stole upon her borrowed ears, and glancing to where the sound came, she saw that the edge of the low cliff was crowded with Small People, who were singing away like a choir of songbirds. Some of them were sitting on Piskey-stools,* some on the edge of the cliff, others were standing. In the background were a score or more of tiny musicians, with reeds, flutes, and other instruments of music in their hands. These last were quaintly dressed in poppy-coloured coats and speedwell-blue breeches, and on their dear little heads were blue three-cornered hats turned up with the same rich colour as their coats. The whole company of Wee Folk were delightful to look at as they were to listen to ; and as for the tiny ladies of the party, they were, Bessie Jane told herself, little nosegays of wildflowers, and if they had not been trilling and

* Mushrooms.

piping as she came upon them, she would have mistaken them for cliff-blossoms, so bright they looked in their lovely gowns of trefoil-gold and reds, thrift-pink, squill-blue, and all those exquisite colours that make the Cornish cliffs so beautiful in the late spring and early summer-time.

'*Bowed like a courtier.*'

The Small People saw the child, and seemed quite pleased to see her, for they smiled most graciously, and one of the little musicians took off his three-cornered hat and bowed like a courtier, and said he hoped she did not mind their singing, as it was their custom to sing a little impromptu song to their cousins—the sea-fairies—every beautiful morning in

May, that being, he told her, the month of flowers and music.

Bessie Jane did not mind in the least. Indeed, she was delighted to think she had come in time to hear one of their little songs, only she was far too shy to say so.

She sat on the cliff where she could see the Wee Folk and Harlyn Bay at the same time. The sea was coming in, and was already under the cliff where she was sitting ; as she looked down into the water she saw it was full of lovely little creatures, who were gazing up at her with all the eyes in their heads. They were sea-fairies, she could tell, by their resemblance to the dear little thing she had caught in her shrimping-net. They all wore little green shifts or shirts, through which their tiny pink bodies glowed like a rose, and all had sun-beamed hair and deep-blue eyes. Some of the sea-fairies were riding on the backs of the waves and tossing tiny spray-balls when she first saw them ; others were darting in and out the sea-ripples as quick as sun-flashes, and playing over the inner bay in waves of light. A short distance out were a hundred or more little female sea-fairies dancing, and as they danced and held each others' hands they looked like tiny garlands of sun-beams. They were dancing to a sweet tune of their own, or perhaps to the music of the sea, which was full of lovely sounds to-day, and colour too—that wonderful ethereal blue which is only seen in a summer's dawn.

Borrowed Eyes and Ears

Whilst Bessie Jane was watching the sea-fairies, and wondering if the little friend she had put back into the sea were amongst them, and if she could see her without eyes, the Wee Folk on the cliff suddenly broke into music and song. The song was so wild and free and the music so sweet that the sea-fairies far out in the bay came close under the cliff and listened with the utmost joy, their tiny faces shining with pleasure, and their small bodies swaying in time to the rhythm of the song. As for the child, she thought it was the loveliest music she had ever heard. The song, which was accompanied by lutes, flutes, and reeds, and by the tapping of tiny feet and clapping of hands, was as follows:

' Sing, sing, sea-fairies, sing !
For the dark has fled
At the dawn's soft tread ;
And the moon grows cold
In the sun's warm gold.
Sing, sing, sea-fairies, sing !

' Sing, sing, sea fairies, sing !
For the sky's dear bird
O'er the waves is heard ;
And the linnet's flute
Like a fairy's lute.
Sing, sing, sea fairies, sing !

' Sing, sing, sea-fairies, sing !
For sandpipers play
By the pools to-day ;
And kittiwakes laugh
As the light they quaff.
Sing, sing, sea-fairies, sing !

Borrowed Eyes and Ears

'Sing, sing, sea-fairies, sing !
  For gulls are afloat
  Like a silver boat ;
  And the curlews call
  As their weird cries fall.
  Sing, sing, sea-fairies, sing !

'Sing, sing, sea-fairies, sing !
  For the waves clap hands
  On the yellow sands ;
  And the sea-sprites dance
  Where the sunbeams glance.
  Sing, sing, sea-fairies, sing !

'Sing, sing, sea-fairies, sing !
  For each little sprite
  Is a rhythm of light ;
  And sweet are their lips
  Like honey-bee's sips !
  Sing, sing, sea-fairies, sing !

'Sing, sing, sea-fairies, sing !
  For day has begun,
  And high is the sun ;
  Now hasten away
  To your dears and play !
  Sing, sing, sea-fairies, sing !'

Bessie Jane held her breath until the music died away in the silver cadence of the morning sea, and the song was still in her ears, so that she was hardly conscious it was finished until she noticed the Small People had risen from the Piskey-stools and were leaving the cliff.

'You aren't going, are you, dear Little People ?'

she cried, forgetting her shyness in her dismay at their going so soon.

'Yes,' answered one of them. 'I hope you liked our song.'

'I did a terrible lot,' responded Bessie Jane, flushing to the roots of her pretty brown hair; 'your singing was lovely, and I should like to hear you sing every morning of my life! It was sweeter even than the thrush's song at sunset, I think.'

The Wee Folk were delighted at the child's praise; the small musicians beamed upon her, and the tiny ladies made her a deep curtsey, and then they all disappeared into the cliff.

She waited ever so long, hoping they would appear again and sing another song, but as they did not, she went down the cliff-path to the beach. At the ending of the song, all the sea-fairies had gone out into the bay to join the merry dancers, who were dancing away like a Bobby Griglan,* she told herself as she sent her glance over the sunlit waters to where they were. When she stood close to the waves all these little whirligigs came dancing shorewards, until they stopped only a few feet away and gazed at her curiously.

When they found their tongues, which they quickly did, to her great delight they began talking to her. They thanked her for being so kind to their little companion in giving her back to them the day before, and said how glad they were she had repaid the

* A fairy.

little girl's kindness in lending Bessie Jane her eyes and ears for a night and a day, as they heard she had so much wanted to see the sea-fairies.

'Yes, I did,' replied Bessie Jane, 'and I am awfully grateful to that pretty little dear for the loan of her ears and eyes, but I am afraid it was very selfish of me to get her to lend them.'

'She was very glad to lend them for the time you asked,' the sea-fairies reassured her—'not only because you did her all that kindness, but because you have been so very good to the poor old Wise Woman, who loves all the Little People, sea-fairies and all,' they said.

It was a great surprise to Bessie Jane that the fairies should know about her kindness to poor Old Annis; and as she did not like being praised, she turned the conversation, and asked the dear little sea-sprites to tell her all about themselves, and what they did all day long, where they lived, and a hundred and one other questions which the sweet-voiced, sun-beamed little creatures seemed only too pleased to answer.

Amongst other interesting things, they told the child about their work. They said their chief happiness was to do good, and that their special work was to seek out all wounded things and take down to the bottom of the sea, where they had a Place of Healing, and where they tended with gentle care all the poor, hurt creatures they found, until they were all healed and happy again. Another mission of theirs was to sing requiems over the poor drowned human beings, and to plant sea-lilies and other sea-flowers on their graves.

They were always busy, they told her, and when there was no special work for them to do they busied themselves with games, singing and dancing, and flashing in and out of the sea to make it beautiful with light. Their special time for merry-making and dancing was at sunset and sunrise, particularly sunset, for then the great sun went down into the sea to shine upon their lovely gardens, parks, and meadows under the sea where they lived, and where dear little fishes sang instead of birds!

It would fill pages to tell all those little sea-fairies told Bessie Jane, and which they told in such entrancing way that time flew. The tide came in and went out, and was again coming in, and the entranced child did not even notice it, or that the big white sun was wheeling down towards his setting.

A great lane of crimson fire stretched away on the blue-grey water from the outer bay to the horizon, and just as the sea-fairies had finished telling her all the wonders of their life and doings she saw coming towards her down this lane of rich light a tiny carriage in the shape of a scallop-shell, drawn by four little horses, two abreast, and white as sea-spray. As the tiny steeds sped onward and drew near, Bessie Jane saw leaning back in the carriage a sea-fairy with a bandage of red seaweed across her eyes and ears.

Borrowed Eyes and Ears

When the horses stopped, all the sea-fairies formed themselves in a circle round the carriage, and looked intently at the child on the shore.

As Bessie Jane noted all this, telling herself what handsome horses they were and what an elegant little carriage, and how beautiful it looked on the sun's pathway, a silvery voice, like the twitter of a baby lark low in its nest amongst the heather, piped from the carriage :

' Please give me back my eyes and my ears.'

' What eyes and ears ?' asked the child, bewildered, for she had quite forgotten that she had got the sea-fairy's eyes and ears.

' Why, my *own* dear little eyes and ears that I lent you for a night and a day,' piped the sweet voice again.

' *Must* I give them back ?' asked Bessie Jane.

' Indeed you must,' said the fairy. ' I have missed them oh so much ! No beautiful vision have I seen, no lovely sounds have I heard, since I lent them to you yesterday afternoon. I waited until the sun had put on his flame-coloured robe before coming for them.'

' How can I give you back your eyes and your ears ?' asked the child helplessly. ' The Wise Woman put them in, and she isn't here to take them out.'

' Say, " Little Blue Eyes, go back to your homes," and, " Little Pink Ears, return to your places," and they will do as you tell them,' answered the little fairy.

Borrowed Eyes and Ears

Bessie Jane, though very reluctant to give back what had given her so much pleasure, knew she would be dreadfully selfish if she did not do as she was told, and after gazing full five minutes on the wonderful sight—the circle of sea-fairies, the wee white horses, and scallop-shaped carriage, the like of which she might never see again—and letting her last gaze rest on her first friend waiting so patiently for the return of her eyes and ears, her clear young voice rang out :

'Dear Little Blue Eyes, go back to your homes ; dear Little Pink Ears, go back to your holes.'

As she spoke a blue spark leapt out of her eyes, followed by a whizzing of something pink, and when she opened her eyes again, the radiant circle of sea-fairies round the mother-of-pearl carriage, the dazzling white steeds with flowing manes and tails, were all gone, and she only saw the usual sights of eventide on the beach : the gulls flying over the hillocks and across the sands to their sleeping-places in the cliffs ; a man driving the cows up the bay to be milked ; the stems of the tamarisk on the hedges, scarlet in the sun-glow ; and the vast luminous sky over it all. Beautiful as everything was, it was not nearly so beautiful, Bessie Jane thought, as were those little sea-fairies and horses on the pathway of crimson fire !

She stood close to the edge of the water till the line of light was gone, and then she turned away from the sea and went up the beach towards

Tamarisk Lane, to tell Old Annis what she had heard and seen.

As she was going up, she met the same old man and his donkeys she had seen the day before. He was coming down for his last pannier of sand. He stopped and spoke to her, and asked why she was looking so happy.

'I have seen the Small People,' answered the child, 'and the dear little fairies that live in the sea.'

'You don't mean to say so?' cried the old man. 'You are a lucky little maid to have seen all they little dears!' as Bessie Jane nodded. ''Tis not often folks do see 'em nowadays; but they did backalong, my mother told me. What was 'em like, Miss Bessie Jane?'

'I cannot stop to tell you now,' said the child. 'It is rather late, and I want to go and see the Wise Woman in Tamerisk Lane. You are late getting sand, arn't you?'

'Iss fy, I be. 'Tis for your father—Maister Rosewarne—and I must make haste and get it. My donkey do want his supper, and so do I.'

Old Annis was at her cottage gate watching for her little friend's return, and when the child came up she listened with the greatest interest to all she had to tell her, and said how pleased she was that she had seen and heard so much.

'It is a reward,' she added, 'for being so kind to a poor lonely old woman.'

Bessie Jane never saw any more of the Little

Borrowed Eyes and Ears

People, and never went shrimping again with the shrimping-net made by a Wise Woman out of Piskey-wool spun by the Small People, for the simple reason she lost the net the day after she saw the dear Wee Folk and the sea-fairies with her borrowed eyes. How she lost it, or where, she did not know, and the Wise Woman, wise as she was, could not tell her. But she was ever afterwards grateful for having seen them, especially the sea-fairies, and she showed her gratitude by being kinder than ever to her poor, lonely old friend.

The Little White Hare

WHEN our great-great-grandmothers were young, a small lad called William John Pendarvey went on a visit to his Great-Aunt Ann, a very silent, austere old maid, who lived by herself in the Vale beautiful of Lanherne.

Great Aunt Ann being old and very quiet, was the last person in the world that a tender-hearted, sensitive little chap as William John was should have gone to stay with.

The house where she lived was rather small and very gloomy, and had nothing nice about it, but it possessed a large and beautiful orchard, protected from the rough and cutting winds by the escarpment of the downs that rose above it and the valley.

But delightful as this orchard was, nobody except

The Little White Hare

Great-Aunt Ann—and she not often—ever went into it, because it was known to be haunted by *something*, in the shape of a little White Hare which had been seen there from time unknown, wandering like a shadow over the grass, and in and out amongst the trees, or sitting motionless at the foot of a blasted apple-tree.

Who or *what* this apparition was nobody could tell, but not a man, woman or child in the Vale, except Great-Aunt Ann, would have gone into that orchard for all they were worth.

Little William John might never have known there was an orchard belonging to the gloomy old house if he had not wandered into a bedroom at the back of the house overlooking the entrance to the orchard and peeped out of the window.

He asked to be allowed to go and play there, as it looked so bright and sunny in its open spaces, but Great-Aunt Ann said : ' Not to-day.'

It was always ' Not to-day ' whenever he asked to go into that orchard, and probably he would never have gone into it at all if the old maid had not occasion one day to go to St. Columb, a small market town three miles from where she lived.

She could not take the boy with her, she said, and so she left him at home to take care of the house.

Looking after a house was not in little William John's line, and Great-Aunt Ann had not been gone more than an hour before he found himself at the small wicket-gate opening into the orchard, where to his joy he saw a great multitude of golden-headed daffadillies rising out of the lowly grass, and a light that was softer than silver moving mysteriously in and out amongst the trees.

The temptation to go into that sun-lighted, fascinating spot was irresistible, and finding the gate unlocked, little William John opened it and went in.

It was the spring of the year, and the spring was late, and there were as yet no carmine buds on the apple trees, but their upper branches were misty with the silvery green of budding leaves. And the pear trees were in virgin whiteness, and so were the plum and cherry trees, which made a shining background to all the yellow lilies in blossom there.

' It makes me feel happy only to be here,' whispered little William John to himself ; ' and oh ! the daffies are making golden dawns under the trees !'

He wandered about to his heart's content, staying his young feet now and then to listen to a blackbird's liquid pipe, and to touch with reverent hand a daffadilly's drooping head, or to watch with puzzled eyes that thing of brightness moving on in front of him amongst the trees and blossoms.

He lost sight of this wandering light when he had gone the length of the orchard ; but he saw it again as he turned across to its top, and when he got close he saw, to his astonishment, it was a little Hare of silvery whiteness.

The Little White Hare

It was sitting on its haunches under the blasted tree, and did not move away as the boy drew near.

A thrill of gladness filled William John's kind young heart at so fair and strange a vision, and his delight was even greater when the small White Hare suffered him to stroke its fur.

'Oh, you *dear* little soft thing!' he cried. 'I am so glad you are not afraid of me; I love all animals, and would not hurt any of them for worlds, nor a hair of your beautiful white coat.'

'I knew you would not,' answered the little White Hare. 'I was sure your heart was gentle and good the moment I saw you.'

'What! Can you talk?' asked little William John in amazement. 'I never knew animals could speak like human beings before. I am so glad you can. It is so nice to have someone to talk to. Nobody hardly ever speaks to me here, and I have felt so lonely.'

'Poor boy!' said the little White Hare; 'I can sympathize with you, for I know what it is to be lonely and have nobody to speak to. You are the first human being who has spoken to me since a wicked Witch turned me into the shape of a hare.'

'What! Are you not *really* a hare?' asked little William John, more and more amazed.

'No,' answered the little creature sadly; 'I am a maiden in the shape of a hare, and I have had to bear the hare-shape ever since the Witch worked a spell

' The small White Hare suffered him to stroke its fur.'

The Little White Hare

upon me, which was back in the days of the " giants." '

' What a shame !' cried the boy. ' Whatever made her turn you into a hare ?'

' She had a spite against me because I would not be wicked like herself.'

' How dreadful of her !' cried little William John indignantly. ' Will you never be able to get back your real shape, you poor little thing ?'

' I am afraid not,' said the little White Hare sadly, ' unless somebody who is *really sorry* for me, and is not *afraid* of me, can find the Magic Horn— by the blast of which Jack the Giant-Killer over-threw the Giant Galligantus and Hocus-Pocus the Conjurer—and blow over me three strong, clear blasts.'

' Where is the Magic Horn ?' asked little William John.

' I do not know the exact spot, but it is buried somewhere in the ruins of an old castle called the Castle of Porthmeor, which is on a cliff above Porth-meor Cove.'

' Why, that old castle is *mine,* or will be, I am told, when I am of age !' cried little William John. ' It is not a great way from where I live, and often I go there to play. I wish I wasn't only a little boy, and could look for the Magic Horn,' he added, after a moment's silence.

' Age is no barrier to your seeking it,' said the little White Hare. ' All that is needed to loosen the wicked old Witch's spell is what I have now told you.'

'Then I will look for the Magic Horn directly I get home,' cried little William John, 'and if I can find it I'll come back and blow it over you, if you think I can.'

'I am sure you can,' answered the little White Hare. 'You must go now, for your Great-Aunt is coming into the valley. It is not wrong to come into this orchard, since she has not forbidden you; but she knows it is haunted by a little White Hare, and is afraid if you see it it will work you harm. So you must be patient with her.'

The Hare vanished as it spoke, and little William John found himself alone with the yellow-headed daffadillies, and the trees and dear little birds, and he soon went back to the house.

'Have you been out anywhere?' asked Great-Aunt Ann, when she had come in and taken off her bonnet.

'Yes, into the orchard,' said the boy truthfully. 'It is a lovely place, full of song-birds and flowers.'

'Was that all you saw there?' she asked anxiously.

'No,' answered little William John again, lifting his clear child-eyes to the stern old maid's. 'I saw trees with snow on them, *and a dear little Hare with fur as white as milk.*'

The old lady shook all over like a wind-tossed leaf when he said that, but she did not scold him or say he ought not to have gone into her orchard, but the next day she sent him home.

At the end of three years William John came again to stay with his Great-Aunt Ann—not that she wanted him, but because his guardian thought the balmy air of the lovely Vale would do him good.

The spring was very early this year, and when William John arrived the daffadillies had gone, and the pear and cherry trees had scattered all their snow-white blossoms on the grass; but the apple flowers were out in rosy splendour on the gnarled old trees, and where the daffadillies had made 'golden dawns' there were blue-grey periwinkles trying to lift themselves to the heavenly blue shining down upon them.

William John was anxious to go out into the orchard directly he came, but Great-Aunt Ann said the grass was too wet.

The grass was always 'too wet,' according to the old maid, and the boy was afraid she would not allow him to go into the orchard at all.

When he had been there two weeks and a day, Great-Aunt Ann had again occasion to go to St. Columb town, and as there was only room in the gig for the driver and herself, she was obliged to leave him at home.

The moment the gig was out of sight William John made his way to the orchard, where he found the grass as green and beautiful as spring grass could be, and his little friend the Hare sitting under the blasted tree, whiter and smaller than ever.

'I began to fear you would never come into this orchard again,' said the White Hare plaintively.

'I began to fear so myself,' responded William John, stroking very gently the little White Hare. 'This is my first opportunity of coming here.'

'Have you found the Magic Horn?' the small creature asked anxiously.

'Not yet, and I have never stopped looking for it since I was last here. I have searched all over the old castle, and every stone has been lifted on the place, and the ground dug up both outside the ruins and inside, and I am afraid the Magic Horn was not hidden away in that old castle, as you said.'

'It *was* hidden there, and is there now,' insisted the little White Hare, 'and I do hope you aren't going to give up looking for it.'

'I won't, for your sake, you dear little soft thing!' cried the boy, and again he stroked her gently and tenderly; 'and as you are sure it is there somewhere, I'll search until I find it.'

'Have you looked in the cave under the castle?' asked the little White Hare.

'No,' returned William John; 'the entrance to it is not known, and even if it were, the passage leading down to the cave is so foul with bad air, my guardian said, that it would be death to anybody who went through it.'

'If you are not afraid to go down into the cave, I

can give you a plant that will purify all the foul air you pass through.'

'I will not be afraid for your sake, dear little White Hare,' said the boy.

The Hare vanished, and in a little while became visible again, and in her mouth she held a strange-looking weed, the like of which he had never seen before.

'It is called the little All-Pure,' said the White Hare, as William John took it in his hand. 'Keep it close to your heart until you have discovered the passage to the cave, and when it is foul hold it in your hand until its brightness shines on the Magic Horn.'

Again she disappeared, and the boy, after waiting some time to see if she would appear again, went back to the house, where he found his Great-Aunt Ann limping in at the front-door.

The old lady had hurt her leg in getting out of the gig, and when he told her he had been in the orchard, she made her slight accident an excuse to send him back to his home, which she did that same day.

William John did not have the chance of paying another visit to his Great-Aunt Ann until he was a youth of nineteen, and he would not have come then if he had waited to be invited.

The old maid was now terribly old and feeble, and had to keep a servant. Unhappily for William John, the servant was quite as crabbed and silent as her mistress, and even more opposed to his going into the old orchard. She even locked the orchard-gate and kept the key in her pocket.

But William John, being now no longer a child, but a handsome youth with a strong will of his own, was determined to get into the orchard with or without permission, for he had found the Magic Horn.

He watched his opportunity, and one day when the servant was out he went to the wicket gate and sprang over it, and quickly made his way to the blasted tree, where he found, as he had expected to find, the little White Hare sitting on her haunches under it.

She was very white and ever so small—so small, in fact, that she did not look much bigger than a baby hare.

'You have come *at last*,' she said, as the tall handsome lad knelt on the grass and caressed her. ' Have you found the Magic Horn ?'

' I have found it,' he answered gladly.

' *When* did you find it ?'

' Only yesterday,' returned the youth. ' Every day since I last saw you I have searched for the entrance to the cave, and at last, when I was in despair of ever finding it, I came upon it under my bedroom window. I discovered it quite by accident, as I was planting maiden-blush rose-trees. I never knew till then that our house was built on the old castle grounds. The passage opened on to steps, which led down and down till they ended at the door of the cave.'

'Were you not afraid?' asked the little White Hare very softly.

'I was a little bit,' confessed the youth, 'for I did not know where it would lead me. But *love* and *pity* for poor little you made me go on. And I had the little All-Pure to cheer me; for it not only made the foul air through which I passed pure and sweet, but gave out a soft clear light. I found the Magic Horn on a slab of stone in the corner of the cave. I took it up quickly and returned the way I came, and started the earliest moment to pay a visit to my Great-Aunt Ann.'

'Have you brought the Magic Horn with you?' asked the little White Hare, with deep anxiety in her voice.

'Yes,' he said, with shining eyes, 'and here it is;' and he laid a black thing in the shape of a horn on the grass beside her.

'*It is the Magic Horn!*' cried the little White Hare joyfully. 'Will you blow over me three strong, clear blasts, dear William John? If you are as pure-hearted as you are kind-hearted, as I am sure you are, the last blast will break the Witch's spell, and give me back my own shape. The Horn should be blown at sunset.'

'It is sundown now,' said William John, looking westward, where between the trees he could see a splendour of rose and gold painted on the lower sky.

The Little White Hare

' Then blow it *now !*' cried the little White Hare ; and stiffening herself on her form, she crossed her paws on her breast and waited.

' *Took up the Magic Horn and put it to his mouth.*'

William John took up the Magic Horn in his strong young hands and put it to his mouth, and in a minute or less there sounded out through the

The Little White Hare

orchard, all gay with apple-blossom and melody of
birds, and over the Vale of Lanherne, a great blast,
so rich in sound that the thrushes stopped their
singing, and the people in St. Mawgan village came
rushing to their doors to know whatever it was.   It
was quickly followed by two more blasts, richer and

' He had not expected to see her half so beautiful.'

louder than the first.   When the last blast had died
away, William John, looking down at the foot of
the blasted tree, saw in the place of the little White
Hare the most beautiful maiden he had ever seen.

The Magic Horn fell from his hand at so lovely a
sight, and he blushed red as the buds clinging in rosy
infancy to the apple-trees, and stammered something

out that he had not expected to see her half so beautiful.

'I am myself now, thanks to you,' laughed the maiden; and William John thought it was the sweetest laugh he had ever heard in all his life. 'I can never be sufficiently grateful for all you have done for me.'

'Mine is the gratitude for having been allowed to find the Magic Horn and loosen you from the wicked spell,' said the lad, still stammering and blushing.

'You are very good to say so,' said the lovely maid, blushing in her turn as she felt the gaze of the handsome youth upon her. 'Now the evil spell has been undone I must go my way.'

'What way?' asked William John eagerly, drinking in the beauty of her face.

'To a country beyond the sun-setting, where all who love me are,' she said gently.

'If you go, I must also go,' said William John in a masterful way, still keeping his eyes on her face. 'I learnt to love you in your hare-shape, dear, but I love you a thousand times more now I see you as you are. I could not live without you now.'

'If you love me as you say you do, and cannot live without me, you may come,' said the lovely maid, lifting her shy eyes to his. 'You have the right to come with me by the good you have wrought. It is a fair land whither I am going, where there are always buds and blossoms on the trees, where the

The Little White Hare

happy birds are always in song, and where the Foot of Evil dare not enter. It is time I was away. The sun is setting, and his path of glory is narrowing on the sea. Come, if you will. *I love you, too,* dear.'

And giving him her little hand, which he gladly took, they went both of them together out of the old orchard in the glow of the setting sun ; and as they climbed a slope above the place of blossoming trees, an old man crossing the downs wondered who that handsome youth and lovely maid were making their way with locked hands and steadfast faces towards the sunset. But he never knew.

From that day onwards the little White Hare was never again seen in the old beautiful orchard, and nobody ever knew what had become of William John.

'*In the glow of the setting sun.*'